The Little Space

Pitt Poetry Series

Ed Ochester, *Editor*

The Little Space

Poems Selected and New,

1968–1998

Alicia Suskin Ostriker

University of Pittsburgh Press

Published by the University of Pittsburgh Press, Pittsburgh, Pa. 15261

Copyright © 1998, Alicia Suskin Ostriker

All rights reserved

Manufactured in the United States of America

Printed on acid-free paper

10 9 8 7 6 5 4 3 2 1

A CIP catalog record for this book is available from the British Library.

Contents

Early Poems (1968–1974)
The Anniversary   3
Excerpts from *Once More Out of Darkness*   4
Wrinkly Lady Dancer   8

A Dream of Springtime (1979)
Becky and Benny in Far Rockaway   11
Sonnet. To Tell the Truth   12
Annie, Aphrodite, and the Elevator   13
Portraite de l'Artiste   15
Portrait of a Man   16
The Fool Stands Up to Teach King Lear Again   17

The Mother/Child Papers (1980)
Cambodia   21
Excerpts from "Mother/Child"   26
Mother/Child: Coda   36
Excerpt from "Propaganda Poem: Maybe for Some
    Young Mamas"   38
The Leaf Pile   39
The Change   41
In the Dust   43
His Speed and Strength   44

A Woman Under the Surface (1982)

The Waiting Room   47

After the Shipwreck   49

The Crazy Lady Speaking   50

The Exchange   51

The History of America   52

Dream: The Disclosure   53

Homecoming   54

The Impulse of Singing   56

Excerpt from "Message from the Sleeper at Hell's Mouth"   57

The Runner   59

A Minor Van Gogh (He Speaks):   61

Waterlilies and Japanese Bridge   62

The Singing School   64

The Imaginary Lover (1986)

Cows   67

Horses   69

Staring at the Pacific, and Swimming in It   71

Three Men Walking, Three Brown Silhouettes   73

Mother in Airport Parking Lot   75

The Marriage Nocturne   77

Surviving   79

Meeting the Dead   86

Listen   88

A Question of Time   90

Years   92

I Brood About Some Concepts, for Example   93

Taking the Shuttle with Franz   95

Everywoman Her Own Theology   97

Poem Beginning with a Line by Fitzgerald/Hemingway   99

The War of Men and Women   103

A Clearing by a Stream   111

Letting the Doves Out   113

Green Age (1989)

Fifty   117

A Young Woman, a Tree   119

Helium   122

George in Hospital   123

Excerpts from "A Birthday Suite"   124

Stream   128

The Pure Products of America   130

Windshield   132

The Bride   133

The Death Ghazals   136

A Meditation in Seven Days   141

Excerpts from "Homage to Rumi"   152

To Love Is   157

Move   159

The Crack in Everything (1996)

The Dogs at Live Oak Beach, Santa Cruz   163

Boil   164

Marie at Tea   166

Migrant   169

Globule   170

Nude Descending   172

The Studio (Homage to Alice Neel)   174

Appearance and Reality   175

The Boys, the Broomhandle, the Retarded Girl   177

The Eighth and Thirteenth   178

Saturday Night   181

The Book of Life   183

Middle-Aged Woman at a Pond   191

The Nature of Beauty   192

The Class   194

Locker Room Conversation   196

Jonah's Gourd Vine   198

Still Life: A Glassful of Zinnias on My Daughter's
    Kitchen Table   199

Excerpts from "The Mastectomy Poems"   202

Uncollected and New Poems (1980–1998)

April One   217

From the Prado Rotunda: The Family of Charles IV,
    and Others   220

A Chinese Fan Painting   222

O'Keeffe   223

Anselm Kiefer   224

Holocaust   225

Diaspora   227

Millennial Polka   228

About Time   229

Acknowledgments   231

Early Poems
(1968–1974)

❧ The Anniversary

Of course we failed, by succeeding.
The fiery cherub becomes his smothering,
A greedy heart dives into a dream
Of power or truth, and wakes up middle aged
In some committee room.
It is eating paper instead of God.
We two are one, my bird, this is a wedding.

When love was war, you swore you'd burn
Your life and die at thirty-five. I said good riddance,
Bright hairy boy, I will beat you, down,
Tear you to monkey shreds, survive like earth,
Owl-eyed, because I wanted to see everything
Black and permanent and kill you with your theories.
We used to wake up sweaty and entangled.

Thirty, home, and work. We cohabit in a functioning machine.
There is violence, somewhere else. Do we wish this? It occurs,
The flayed combatant, the dismembered child,
The instruments in the basement. We must wish it. See,
Between us is peace, our babies are plump,
I know you, I caress you, I fail you. My faith adheres
In nothing. Don't leave me, don't leave me.

✑ Excerpts from *Once More Out of Darkness*

> For we are put on earth a little space
> That we may learn to bear the beams of love.
> — *William Blake*

✑

Once more out of darkness
Come the great green hills.
Wind plunges and lifts,
Jays plunge and scream overhead.
Slowly erupts up
Again the risen red.

✑

The supposed virgins sitting in a circle
Under old portraits of Margaret Sanger
Are here to receive their first, new, innocent diaphragms;
I, however, am their fabled goddess.
I am conducted to the sanctuary, I submit to indignities;
Skirt up, feet in stirrups, one look, one rotating poke—
Examination of the entrails? Quite right, due process,
Good cow. "Five weeks," the voice intones. "Hooray,"
I say, and pay (the dogfaced nurses cheerful)
And get to a phone fast, pretending to be
(In the shabby drugstore) Western Union, a singing telegram,
"Love, oh love, oh careless love," it sings, "you see
What Love has done to me," and hang up giggling.

Consequence: Join the world, which is full
Of ballooning mamas and baffled but willing papas
For future communion. We join it. We toss
Off quarts of milk, we invent spinach recipes
To rectify the diet, we observe the tenderness
Of my breasts, and that I pee more and sleep more
And weep more; by which signs alone is made known
The invisible change, the silent grafting-on
Or addition of an infinity, the implausible, actual
Shift of the peopled universe, for which we are

Responsible. Nevertheless, my foetus, I cannot picture
You yet. Are you thumb-length? A fish? Have you a tail?
Are you hairy? Will I be good to you?
Archangel Spock, Guttmacher, Grantley Dick-Read,
Pray for us now, we follow your lead.

≈

Therefore a swollen freighter
Moving without will
Pursues its nature still.
    The waves go by,
    What freight have I?
    It is daylight
    It is even
    It is the world's night
      Travel forward
      Insensible barrow, pilgrim
Laden:

≈

And I saw Jerusalem descending, a city yet a woman
Twelve gates, and the brightness
From everlasting to everlasting. Now:
For her outsides, car-dumps, motel strips,
For her inside, sewer slums, brain of phone wires,
  edifices of municipal troglodyte, the greased
  slide of paste restaurant, urine movie, puke dancehall
  meths subway sleep, pus alley . . . rat hunger . . .
Over an empty road you drove
To the brim of a town
Where shone in the darkness four signs: FOOD. BEAUTY.
  GAS. DRUGS.
Her eyes are the suburbs

Decent
I want to be decent
In the bath, sweet hills and valleys
Afloat, suspended, miraculous
Mountain land, grazing land, building land, planting land
Wander here with me
In a dream on that ancient sea
That large lump, there the life lies. But:
Doctor, I have one breast pointing down and one breast pointing up.
Doctor, my veins are like hoses.
Give me something. I cannot sleep for the kicking.
I worry. I think there will be pain. What then.
What to do. I grow old even as I tell you this.
Ugly
You cannot deny it is ugly

For each day as I wait
The papers making hate
The dope box bleating
Bombs mute, the movie
Screen removing its clothes
Turn me weary, weary
Of time, gyrating
I follow my groove
Washing teaspoons, picking
Up old chicken bones, dragging
My sheets flat, netted, assailed,
Do your dainties have that soiled
Look, it bubbles, it flows.
Let him who is pure
Descend his mire.
Let the official coward
Move nations backward and forward.
I am making this child for you:
Brown pot of my body
Spatula of his body

And vowed minds, damned all
From love's beginning either
To be "unfaithful" or to be "faithful,"
That is to rot by
The gaudy wicked lie or the mean inhibited lie,
Came once together
As in the promise.

From the sweat of this,
Male and female vessel
Whirling cracked on the wheel:
      For you:
Of the dripping wound
Of the walls of insanity
Of proud man's contumely, of law's delay
Of fire, famine, age,
Ague, tyranny,
(Did any, on the way,
Spew a babe, on the way to the chambers?
What did the soldiers say?)
Old men that pray in the oven's mouth,
Ancestral grief of woman,
All shrieks to heaven from the battered down,
    Whoever has died, I make this child for you.

✇ Wrinkly Lady Dancer

Going to be an old wrinkly lady
Going to be one of those frail rag people
Going to have withered hands and be
Puzzled to tears crossing the street

Hobble cautiously onto buses
Like a withery fruit
And quite silently sitting in this lurching bus
The avenues coming by

Some other passengers gaze at me
Clutching my cane and my newspaper
Seemingly protectively, but I will really be thinking about
The afternoon I danced naked with you
The afternoon I danced naked with you
The afternoon! I danced! Naked with you!

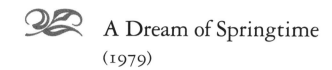 A Dream of Springtime

(1979)

✍ Becky and Benny in Far Rockaway

Near the Atlantic Ocean, past the last subway station,
Streaks of sand on the sidewalk,
Armies of aging Jews, soaking up sun
As if it were Talmud,
And the rickety white stairs
To an apartment like a frail body.

My uncle and aunt were both warty, like alligators.
They set a lunch on the oilcloth-covered table.
I felt peculiar about the smells.

The lunch seemed to go on all afternoon,
Anxious syllables fluttering over my head like fireflies.
Shayne Maydel was me.
Eat, they said in English, eat.
So I ate, and finally reached the pastoral scene,
Bo Peep, pink roses, green leaves
At the dish bottom,
One of those sweet, impossible memories
Jews used to buy themselves in America.

The two of them beamed,
Gold-toothed, as if their exile were canceled.
You should eat and be healthy, they said.

Sonnet. To Tell the Truth

To tell the truth, those brick Housing Authority buildings
For whose loveliness no soul had planned,
Like random dominoes stood, worn out and facing each other,
Creating the enclosure that was our home.

Long basement corridors connected one house to another
And had a special smell, from old bicycles and baby carriages
In the storage rooms. The elevators
Were used by kissing teenagers.

The playground—iron swingchains, fences, iron monkey bars,
Iron seesaw handles, doubtless now rusted—
Left a strong iron smell on my hands and in the autumn air
And rang with cries. To me it is even precious

Where they chased the local Mongoloid, yelling "Stupid Joey!
                                               Stupid Joey!"
Now I've said everything nice I can about this.

🙖 Annie, Aphrodite, and the Elevator

Annie was some years older, so I trusted,
As still I would, her wisdom.
She went to Sacred Heart, where the nuns beat you,
But wore that shield, pierceless gentility,
And blond fluctuating hair.

She had this freckled brother, and one winter
Intriguing weeks went by, until at last
The long-expected messages wafted
As if on wings—He wants to be your boyfriend—
He wants to kiss you.
I said: "I'll ask my mother."
My mother's reply, so ambiguous I couldn't understand a word,
Concluded: "Use your judgment."

I used my judgment in the elevator.
We were ladylike—Annie and me—in the elevator,
Ardently resisting, then submitting,
Like in the movies. Tommy's face came close,
Patchy and porous, and I shut my eyes.
We rubbed our lips together, hard as we could, as hard as nails,
As hard as porcelain shepherdess and shepherd.
To me he smelled rusty, like an old frying pan.
But Annie and her boyfriend were truly in love.
She'd said: "He's such a gentleman,"
"I'd like to give myself," and "He respects me."
I could easily see they did it the right way,
And how sustained and wonderful that was,
As we rode to Five in the elevator.
Numerous times we ascended and descended.
That was the winter's tale,

And it was springtime when they finished the walkway
Over the East River Drive . . . we wanted to try it.
The bridge was empty, except for a man in brown

Who seemed to glance at us, wrote something
On the railing, then sauntered down the ramp, toward the river.
He certainly looked bad, so we rushed over. It said:
FUCK YOU IN YOUR HOT RED JUICY BLOODY CUNTS
—And a phone number. We breathed, giggled, and fled.
What did he mean? I wondered, while Annie
Stared at me, smiled, and shook her shining head.

✷ Portraite de l'Artiste

When everybody's in bed
And you are away,
I'm alone, working on woodcuts,
Accompanied by a radio.
I print, revise, print,
I lay the ricepaper in rows on shelves.
I am trying, in this print,
To represent, simultaneously,
Two smoothed stones, such as one finds by the ocean;
Fruit—a pear for example;
And a torso, divided by a backbone and containing
A curled foetus. The colors
Are grays and pink oranges. I try also
To retain the wood grain.
The night is cold.
Meanwhile the hands on my watch
Go around and around.
Later I draw myself, with the baby inside me,
Standing in a long mirror,
Portraite de l'artiste enceinte,
Ugly, proud, dignified,
Good bones after all,
Peaceful.

I think, "I was born lonely. I am best so."
And an artist at work can always
Be accompanied by death, which is happy.
But after all,
Most of my nights I spend with your hot body,
First making love, then curled together,
Then rolling around back to back, pajamaless,
Which, we have decided, or discovered, is best for sleeping
The whole night through—
I think my mother and father slept the same way, if
I remember correctly—
Even in sleep, not separated.

✎ Portrait of a Man

You wear glasses.
You wear blue flannel pajamas.
You are doing calculations on an envelope, and as you pause to think,
The lamp shines on your hands.
Here is your work, that you love
With a mad, faunlike, hidden mind,
Inherited from Pythagoras,
From Al-Jabr, from Descartes, from God knows who.
Very well.
Your profile, toward me, is not
Smooth as in boyhood.
Very well.
Our heating system hums and rattles
Against the November weather
That presses chillingly up
From our backyard at the windowglass.
Some Ravel piano piece storms on the radio
Filling the room with intangible turbulences.
Like nested birds, our children sleep upstairs
Not yet formed, but forming, becoming strangers.
Very well.
As for me, man, I'm watching your loneliness.
Making a portrait of you.
Of you, who do not wish
To think of the winter approaching
With its wet black wings.

The light outlines
Serviceably the bumps
And indentations of your face and hands.
You rub your blackhaired chest, under the pajamas.
Why this invisible dance? This faithful striving for clarity?
Will our scratches, in fact, correspond to the starry whirl?
Ravel elaborates his terms of climax.
Having cogitated, you begin again to write.

The Fool Stands Up to Teach King Lear Again

—In memory of Paul Goodman

The systematic murder of the young
Before they reach me, by stupid and crippled elders,
The bland, blank-faced rejection of their own
Depths, by the secret terror that nails them
To hold very still, praying not to be seen
By the teacher, each other, themselves—
Baffles me. Ripeness is all. I think of those classroom walls
Painted quite to resemble stale vomit.
There they sit; and among them the still
Intelligent and eager, the green fruit
That well may well rot before we ripen it.

Furthermore: consider my incompetence, my laziness, my
Inability to tell jokes. Why
Should anybody listen? O failure! failure!
My stomach flutters and jams, I am terrified
Of knowing nothing, except that beauty is truth—
Useless, and the wrong poet. Then once more,
None does offend—none! I say none! I'll able 'em,
Yells the mad king, who ables us. *Come, boy—*
I rush in late, open the book, stand there:
All I can do is demonstrate my joy.

The Mother/Child Papers

(1980)

❧ Cambodia

My son Gabriel was born on May 14, 1970, during the Vietnam War, a few days after the United States invaded Cambodia, and a few days after four students had been shot by National Guardsmen at Kent State University in Ohio during a protest demonstration.

On May 1, President Nixon announced Operation Total Victory, sending 5,000 American troops into Cambodia to destroy North Vietnamese military sanctuaries, in a test of "our will and character," so that America would not seem "a pitiful helpless giant" or "accept the first defeat in its proud 190-year history."

He wanted his own war.
> The boy students stand in line
> at Ohio State
> each faces a guardsmen in a gasmask
> each a bayonet point at his throat.

U.S. air cavalry thrusts into Kompong Cham province, seeking bunkers. Helicopters descend on "The Parrot's Beak." B-52's heavily bomb Red sanctuaries. Body count! Body count high! in the hundreds. The President has explained, and explains again, that this is not an invasion.

Monday, May 4th, at Kent State, laughing demonstrators and rock throwers on a lawn spotted with dandelions. It was after a weekend of beerdrinking. Outnumbered Guardsmen, partially encircled and out of tear gas, begin to retreat uphill, turn, kneel, in unison aim their guns. Four students lie dead, seventeen wounded. 441 colleges and universities strike, many shut down.

The President says: "When dissent turns to violence, it invites tragedy."

A veteran of Khe Sanh says: "I saw enough violence, blood and death and I vowed never again, never again . . . Now I must protest.

I'm not a leftist but I can't go any further. I'll do damn near anything to stop the war now."

A man in workclothes tries to seize an American flag from a student. "That's my flag! I fought for it! You have no right to it! . . . To hell with your movement. We're fed up with your movement. You're forcing us into it. We'll have to kill you." An ad salesman in Chicago: "I'm getting to feel like I'd actually enjoy going out and shooting some of these people, I'm just so goddamned mad."

One, two, three, four, we don't want! your fucking war!
They gather around the monument, on the wet grass, Dionysiac, beaded, flinging their clothes away. New England, Midwest, South-west, cupfuls of innocents leave the city and buy farmland. At the end of the frontier, their backs to the briny Pacific, buses of tourists gape at the acid-dropping children in the San Francisco streets. A firebomb flares. An electric guitar bleeds.

Camus: "I would like to be able to love my country and still love justice."

Some years earlier, my two daughters were born, one in Wisconsin at a progressive university hospital where doctors and staff behaved af-fectionately, one in England where the midwife was a practical woman who held onto my feet and when she became impatient with me said: PUSH, Mother. Therefore I thought I knew what childbirth was supposed to be: a woman *gives birth* to a *child,* and the medical folk assist her.

But in the winter of 1970 I had arrived five months pregnant in Southern California, had difficulty finding an obstetrician who would take me, and so was now tasting normal American medical care. It tasted like money. During my initial visit to his ranch-style offices on a street where palm trees lifted their heads into the smog like a row of fine mulatto ladies, Dr. Keensmile called me "Alicia" repeatedly, brightly, benignly, as if I were a child or a servant. I hated him right away. I hated his suntan. I knew he was untrue to his wife. I was sure he played golf. The routine delivery anesthetic for him and his group was a spinal block, he said. I explained that I would not need a spinal since I had got by before on a couple of cervical shots, assumed that deliveries were progressively easier, and wanted to decide about drugs myself when the time came. He smiled tolerantly at the ceiling. I remarked that I liked childbirth. I remarked that childbirth gave a woman an opportunity for supreme pleasure and heroism. He smiled again. They teach them, in medical school, that pregnancy and birth are diseases. He twinkled. Besides, it was evident that he hated women. Perhaps that is why he became an obstetrician. Just be sure and watch your weight, Alicia. Smile.

I toyed, as I swelled and bulged like a watermelon, with the thought of driving out into the Mohave to have the baby. I continued my visits to Dr. Keensmile. I did not talk to Dr. Keensmile about Cambodia. I did not talk to him about Kent State. *Sauve qui peut.* You want a child of life, stay away from psychic poison. In the waiting room I found pamphlets which said that a newborn baby must be fed on a strict schedule, as it needed the discipline, and that one must not be moved by the fact that it would cry at first, as this was good for it, to start it out on the right foot. And my daughters were laughing at me for my difficulty in buckling their sandals.

In labor, I discovered that I could have an enjoyable time if I squatted on the bed, rocked a little while doing my breathing exercises, and sang songs in my head. The bed had muslin curtains drawn around it; nobody would be embarrassed by me. So I had settled into a mantra and had been traveling downstream with it for some long duration, when a nurse came through the curtains, stork white, to ask if I was ready for my shot. Since the pains were becoming strong and I felt unsure about keeping control through the transitional stage of labor, which is the hardest, I said fine, expecting a local. This would temporarily alleviate the pain of the fast-stretching cervix, leaving other muscles free.

Of course, it was a sedative. I grew furry. They lay me down. I was eight fingers dilated, only five or seven minutes away from the final stage of labor, where a woman needs no drugs because she becomes a goddess. Then Dr. Keensmile appeared to ask me if I was ready for my spinal. A faint flare of "no" passed like a moonbeam. Because of the Demerol, if they had asked me if I was ready to have my head severed, I probably would have said yes. Drool ran from my mouth. Yes, I said.

When they wheeled me to the delivery room, I fought to maintain wakeful consciousness despite the Demerol, and fought to push, with my own body, to give birth to my child myself, despite the fact that I could feel nothing—nothing at all—below the waist, as if I did not exist there, as if I had been cut in half and bandaged.

A stainless place. I am conscious, only my joy is cut off. I feel the stainless will of everyone. Nothing red in the room. I feel myself sweat.

The black-haired head, followed by the supple limbs, emerges in the mirror. The doctor says it is a boy. Three thoughts fall, like file cards. One: Hooray! We made it! Finito! Two: YOU SONOFABITCHING BASTARD, NEXT TIME I'M GOING TO DO THIS RIGHT. Three: What next time?

Our bodies and our minds shoot into joy, like trees into leaves. Playfulness as children, sex, work with muscles, work with brains. Some bits survive, where we are lucky, or clever, or we fight. The world will amputate what it can, wanting us cripples. Cut off from joy, how many women conceive? Cut off, how many bear? And cut, how many give birth to their children? Now I am one of them. I did not fight. Beginning a day after my son's birth, and continuing for a week, I have swordlike headaches, which I attribute to the spinal. I am thirty-three. In the fall I will be back at work, back East. My husband and I have two daughters, both all right so far, and now the son for whom we were hoping. There will never be a next time.

What does this have to do with Cambodia?

❧ Excerpts from "Mother/Child"

The Guards kneeled, they raised their weapons, they fired
into the crowd to protect the peace. There was a sharp orange-red
explosion, diminished by the great warm daylight, a match scratching,
a whine, a tender thud, then the sweet tunnel, then nothing.
Then the tunnel again, the immense difficulty, pressure, then the head
finally is liberated, then they pull the body out.

was dreaming
water was
      falling and
      rising all
         along could
         not see then
            a barrier a
            color red then
                  cold and
                  very afraid

They hoist it, shining, they support it, under artificial lights, under
the neck and knees, it is limp as a glove, a handful of tendrils,
the mother watches it inhale and flex, the bloodclot over the navel
already brown, the father is blushing, he notices how the genitals
nod and bob, ornamental and puffy, mushrooms and ladyslipper,
do you hear this fellow yell now, smiles the doctor, he'll be a soldier.

They have wiped the flesh, it becomes a package, they wheel it away,
    clean
and alone, the mother rests on a plump pillow and is weeping
in the pretty room, her breasts are engorged, she is filling with
    desire,
she has thrown a newspaper to the floor, her television is dark, her
intention is to possess this baby, this piece of earth, not to surrender
a boy to the ring of killers. They bring him, crying. Her throat leaps.

it hurts   it is impossible
            to stop the pain
            it is impossible
        come when it happens

                        please come when it happens

                                    please

I come the way that
moon comes, stars, the tides,
it is involuntary, only

God knows what elastic
pulls me to his hunger, what laws
make me gaze at that pink

forehead as if it were quite
transparent, as if I could see
what is happening daily, the way

       everything is getting attached, getting
       hooked up there
       in his head, the way they are throwing

       a settlement together, with real streets,
       a marketplace, buying and selling, and outside
       the town the ground to break,

       the people sowing and harvesting,
       already planning a city, and I
       want to see it, I want to.

one   is   inside

but things take shape

vanish but reappear

That is   beautiful

The door clicks. He returns to me.
He brings fresh air in.
We kiss, we touch. I am holding the flannel-wrapped baby.
The girls run to him.

He takes his jacket off and waltzes
the weightless
bundle over his shoulder.
We eat dinner, and evening falls.

I have bathed the girls. I walk by our broad bed.
Upon it rests a man
in a snow white shirt, like a great sleepy bird.
Next to him rests his seed, his son.

Lamplight falls on them both. If a woman looks, at such
a sight, is the felt pang
measureless pleasure?
Is it measureless pain?

Here is the strong one, the other   one
Here is the strong one, the other   after the other

Here is the strong one, the other   after the other
Here is the strong one, the other   after

A glass pane toward the spectral, mysterious garden,
a Santa Ana wind through the live-oaks,
ammonia pungent in the nostrils,
no sunrise yet. You lay on the changing table,
meowing, wet. I made you naked, laying
nightgown fabric aside, kissing your neck,
your feet, your ribs, the powdery skin-creases.
You kicked and waved your thin arms, randomly.
My face being down, then, while I was blind,
somebody's hand quietly grasped my hand.
When I looked up
it was you, laughing
laughing!
      a power
such as flew out
         and nearly knocked me over
through your staring eyes
intense, impersonal, like icy dawn
      like the son of beauty, the bow bent, and the arrows drawn—

         as once in midday three white clouds raced
         right across the zenith of the bright blue sky
         a wild west wind
         ripped at their edges like cotton, and they flew—

         outside a white cat jumps
         from a garden fence, glides
         through the yellow grass

yet but a naked, helpless kicking one—

         you were those things
         I saw! and I have seen.
         I shall be singing this
         when all the forests you have burned are green.

I can   do what   I want

Overturn
this body

☙ Mother/Child: Coda

Fear teaches nothing
                that is my message
but O to grow means pain
means division
the crust cracks and the open
                    organism faces danger
    the grass plant bladed and seeded, the forked spruce
      burst from the mountain's northern side that never
        asked to breathe, here in this cold, but must.

    It is the oldest, saddest story.
    The oceans were ebbing.
    The climate was chilling.
    Anyone who had a lung was forced
    to live, not die.
    Anyone who had a leg was forced
    to leap. The driven soldiers of the cause.
      March. Think. Pay no attention to
      the corpses. Do not attempt to join them.
      March. Your task is to survive. You
      are permitted to feel triumph.

    Here is water, here is dry land,
    up there the kingly sky and queenly moon,
    a desire to turn back and a desire
    to go on are the permanent
    instructions, and we know that this has something
    to do with our souls, also that "go on"
    for any individual thing or creature
    at first means "play," "multiply," "strike
    deep, aim straight" and "trust," but that
    later this changes and means "it is too late,"
    "take your last journey," "we love you, but goodbye."
    We do not know yet what the instructions signify
    for an entire species, a muddy ooze,

and we cannot make any prognosis on those levels
or answer the intimate question
                    shall all life
       perish like us, the perfect crest subside?

I am glad and sorry to give you this information.
I see you know it already.
I want to tell you it is not your fault.
It is your fault.

So from now on you are responsible.
That is what we mean when we say
consciousness is a curse.

   Meanwhile we are looking into
   each other's eyes, windows of homes,
   and touching, with sweet pleasure,
   each other's downy surfaces.
   You will never forget this,
   will always seek, beyond every division,
   a healing of division, renewed touch.
          You see the silver bridge
          spanning a flood?
   This is what we mean when we say
   consciousness is a blessing.

❧ Excerpt from "Propaganda Poem: Maybe for Some Young Mamas"

Postscript to Propaganda

That they limit your liberty, of course,
entirely. That they limit your cash. That they limit your sleep.
Your sleep is a dirty torn cloth.
That they whine until you want to murder them. That their beauty
prevents you. That their eating and excreting exactly resembles
the slime-trails of slugs. On your knees you follow, cleaning,
unstaining. That they burn themselves, lacerate themselves, bruise
themselves. That they get ill. That you sit at their bedsides
exhausted, coughing, reading dully to them, wiping their foreheads
with wet washcloths to lower the fever, your life peeling away
from you like layers of cellophane. Of course.

That you are wheels to them. That you are grease.
An iron doorway they kick open, they run out, nobody has
remembered to close it. That their demanding is a gray north wind.
That their sullenness is a damp that rots your wood, their
malice a metal that draws your blood, their disobedience the fire that
burns your sacred book, their sorrows the webbing that entraps you
like a thrashing fish. That when your child grieves, mother,
you bend and grieve. That you disentwine yourself from them, lock
the pores of your love, set them at a distance. That in this
fashion the years pass, like calendar pages flipped in a silent
movie, and you are old, you are wrinkled as tortoises.

Come on, you daughters of bitches, do you want to live forever?

🐚 The Leaf Pile

Now here is a typical children's story
that happens in gorgeous October
when the mothers are coming
in the afternoon, wearing brisk boots
and windy skirts to pick up
the little children from the day care center

Frost in the air
the maples golden and crimson
my son in a leaf pile in the playground dreaming
I am late, the playground is almost
empty, my husband will kill me

I gather my son to go home,
he forgets his sweater in the playground and I send him back
he dawdles, he is playing with leaves
in his mind, it is already a quarter
to six, will you come on I say

and hurry along the corridor, there are yellow and blue rocket
paintings, but I feel bad and ask what did you do today,
do you recognize this story, the way he stands and picks
his nose, move I say, do you want dinner or not
I'm going to make a nice dinner, fried chicken
I wheedle, so could you please walk a little
faster, okay, I walk a little faster and get upstairs
myself, pivot on boot-heel, nobody there,
he is putting something in his mouth, his sable eyelashes
downcast, and I am swooping down the stairwell screaming

damn you
that's filthy
I told you not before dinner

We are climbing the stairs
and I am crying, my son is not crying

I have shaken him, I have pried the sweet from his cheek
I have slapped his cheek like a woman slapping a carpet
with all my strength

    mothers are very strong
    he is too young to do anything about this
    will not remember he remembers it

The mind is a leaf pile where you can bury
anything, pain, the image of a woman
who wears a necklace of skulls, a screaming woman
you dig quickly and deposit the pulpy thing
you drop leaves on it and it stays there, that is the story

    that is sticking in my mind as we push
    the exit door, and run through the evening wind
    to my car where I jerk the gearshift and pick
    up a little speed, going along
    this neat suburban avenue full of maples
    the mark of my hand a blush on my son's cheek.

✒ The Change

Happening now! it is happening
now! even while, after these
gray March weeks—
when every Saturday you drive
out of town into the country
to take your daughter to her riding lesson
and along the thin curving road you peer
into the brown stuff—
still tangled, bare, nothing
beginning.

Nothing beginning, the mud,
the vines, the corpse-like trees
and their floor of sodden leaves unaltered,
oh, you would like to heave
the steering wheel from its socket
or tear your own heart out, exasperated—
that it should freeze and thaw,
then freeze again, and that
no buds have burst, sticky,
deep red, from their twigs—

You want to say it to your daughter.
You want to tell her also how the gray
beeches, ashes and oaks here on Cherry Hill Road
on the way to her riding school
feel the same, although they cannot
rip themselves up by the roots, or run about raving,
or take any action whatever, and are almost dead
with their wish to be alive,
to suck water, to send force through their fibers,
and to change! to change!

Your daughter, surly, unconversational,
a house locking its doors against you,

pulls away
when you touch her shoulder, looks out the window.

You are too old. You remind her of frozen mud.
Nevertheless it is happening, the planet
is swimming toward the sun
like a woman with naked breasts. She cannot help it.
Can you sense, under the ground, the great melting?

⚘ In the Dust

This year, she announces to us all at dinner,
in ballet class she has discovered "perfection."
At the swimming pool all day she practices dives,
stretches out on her towel
like an array of astronomical sensors.
She reads *The Great Gatsby,* cries. It is deep summer,

it is blazing August. I read, I write poems, I make
moist love with my husband, quarrel with him, cry,
make turbulent love. He tends the garden,
she is polite to me. August,
heat, dust. When I wash her hair, I want to run
my hands over her nude body, her readiness.

On the birthday morning we drive to the jeweler's
in the jeweled August sun. She takes my hand
to cross the bright street, asking if it will hurt,
and I say it will sting
like a doctor's needle. She runs ahead to the shop,
where the bearded jeweler punctures her lobes.

It is evening. We are carrying
dishes, glasses and wrappings in from the garden,
wearing our long skirts, saying the party was nice.
Her girlfriends came and admired her fourteen carat
studs, and they played sedately.
Now she lingers and rubs her feet in the grass.

What is that whirling in the dust?
What is that powerful
movement, everywhere, so rapid she cannot see it?
The fireflies are making their phosphorus, slow circles,
the appletrees ripening, and she
is going willingly. I send her willingly.

✂ His Speed and Strength

His speed and strength, which is the strength of ten
years, races me home from the pool.
First I am ahead, Niké, on my bicycle,
no hands, and the *Times* crossword tucked in my rack,
then he is ahead, the Green Hornet,
buzzing up Witherspoon,
flashing around the corner to Nassau Street.

At noon sharp he demonstrated his neat
one-and-a-half flips off the board:
Oh, brave. Did you see me, he wanted to know.
And I doing my backstroke laps was Juno
Oceanus, then for a while I watched some black
and white boys wrestling and joking, teammates, wet
plums and peaches touching each other as if

it is not necessary to make hate,
as if Whitman was right and there is no death.
A big wind at our backs, it is lovely, the maple boughs
ride up and down like ships. Do you mind
if I take off, he says. I'll catch you later,
see you, I shout and wave, as he peels
away, pedaling hard, rocket and pilot.

 A Woman Under the Surface

(1982)

The Waiting Room

We ladies in the Waiting Room of the Atchley Pavilion
Of the Columbia Presbyterian Medical Center
Range in age from the early thirties to the sixties.
We are wearing our tweeds, our rings. The carpet is beige.

Beige walls, beige soundproofed ceilings, beige sofas surround us.
Geometric design of a room divider, wrought iron, to separate
The reception area from the waiting area,
To suggest, gently, that sterility means peace.

Outside, the day is brilliant, windy, and bittercold.
We have come through this weather, but now it does not exist.
We think of our breasts and cervixes.
We glance, shading our eyelids, at each other.

I am wondering what would be a fully human
Way to express our fears, these fears of the betrayal
Of our bodies. How we rely on this machine of flesh:
Dearer than friends, than lovers, than our own thoughts

Can be, it is loyal to us. That without notice it may
Grow subversive seems intolerable, an uprising of house-slaves
Who have always belonged to the family and accomplished
Their tasks discreetly, ever since we were born.

Perhaps we should dress less expensively
And not so well disguise the skeleton. Perhaps
We should sit more closely, ladies, to each other,
On couches arrange to form a circle, upholstered

Some vivid color. Perhaps we should sit on the floor.
They might have music for us. A woman dancer
Might perform, in the center of the circle. What would she do?
Would she pretend to rip the breasts from her body?

From behind a wall, we hear a woman's voice
Screaming. It simply screams. One person
In the waiting room has turned around. Her false
Sooty eyelashes have opened wide.

A few minutes later the screaming has stopped
And the woman in false eyelashes (I see she is very
Pretty, with black long hair, white blouse with bright
Tropical design on sleeves) has lit a cigarette.

෨ After the Shipwreck

Lost, drifting, on the current, as the sun pours down
Like syrup, drifting into afternoon,

The raft endlessly rocks, tips, and we say to each other:
Here is where we will store the rope, the dried meat, the knife,

The medical kit, the biscuits, and the cup.
We will divide the water fairly and honestly.

Black flecks in the air produce dizziness.
Somebody raises a voice and says: Listen, we know there is land

Somewhere, in some direction. We must know it.
And there is the landfall, cerulean mountain-range

On the horizon: there in our minds. Then nothing
But the beauty of ocean,

Numberless waves like living, hysterical heads,
The sun increasingly magnificent,

A sunset wind hitting us. As the spray begins
To coat us with salt, we stop talking. We try to remember.

The Crazy Lady Speaking

I was the one in the IRT tunnel
Rummaging in my patent-leather pocketbook
While deep blue lights flew by the subway window.
You hated my stockings, rolled to the knee.

I was the one in the cafeteria at 2 A.M
My eyes were flat pennies and stared at your plate.
To you it was worse than India.
You were afraid I might urinate on the floor.

I was the one in the faded sweater
Missing three buttons, my hair dyed pumpkin,
At the baseball game in August,
Yelling behind you, getting spit in your hair.

I have all of the rings and necklaces
I need. My apartment smells of cat.
I want to invite you to it. What I approach
Grows like a jungle. I am the one who loves you.

You should have seen me dance in *La Sylphide,*
In *Lac des Cygnes*. You should have seen
My Cleopatra, my Camille, my Juliet.
From each of their graves I rise, daughter. Embrace me.

❦ The Exchange

I am watching a woman swim below the surface
Of the canal, her powerful body shimmering,
Opalescent, her black hair wavering
Like weeds. She does not need to breathe. She faces

Upward, keeping abreast of our rented canoe.
Sweet, thick, white, the blossoms of the locust trees
Cast their fragrance. A redwing blackbird flies
Across the sluggish water. My children paddle.

If I dive down, if she climbs into the boat,
Wet, wordless, she will strangle my children
And throw their limp bodies into the stream.
Skin dripping, she will take my car, drive home.

When my husband answers the doorbell and sees
This magnificent naked woman, bits of sunlight
Glittering on her pubic fur, her muscular
Arm will surround his neck, once for each insult

Endured. He will see the blackbird in her eye,
Her drying mouth incapable of speech,
And I, having exchanged with her, will swim
Away, in the cool water, out of reach.

The History of America

—for Paul Metcalf

A linear projection: a route. It crosses
The ocean in many ships. Arriving in the new
Land, it cuts through and down forests and it
Keeps moving. Terrain: Rock, weaponry.
Dark trees, mastery. Grass, to yield. Earth,
Reproachful. Fox, bear, coon, wildcat
Prowl gloomily, it kills them, it skins them,
Its language alters, no account varmint, its
Teeth set, nothing defeats its obsession, it becomes
A snake in the reedy river. Spits and prays,
Keeps moving. Behind it, a steel track. Cold,
Permanent. Not permanent. It will decay. This
Does not matter, it does not actually care,
Murdering the buffalo, driving the laggard regiments,
The caring was a necessary myth, an eagle like
A speck in heaven dives. The line believes
That the entire wrinkled mountain range is the
Eagle's nest, and everything tumbles in place.
It buries its balls at Wounded Knee, it rushes
Gold, it gambles. It buys plastics. Another
Ocean stops it. Soon, soon, up by its roots,
Severed, irrecoverably torn, that does not matter,
It decides, perpendicular from here: escape.

A prior circle: a mouth. It is nowhere,
Everywhere, swollen, warm. Expanding and contracting
It absorbs and projects children, jungles,
Black shoes, pennies, blood. It speaks
Too many dark, suffering languages. Reaching a hand
Toward its throat, you disappear entirely. No
Wonder you fear this bleeding pulse, no wonder.

Dream: The Disclosure

> Now we see through a glass darkly, but
> Then face to face: here I know in part but
> there I shall know even as I am known.
> —*Corinthians 13:12*

If I would further than I have
Passionately disclosed/disclothed to you
The purple shapes fruits under my skin

    and if we were to lift my unneeded skin
    to discover these convexities—
    pointing the finger, as if we are in biology—

The organs in their refreshing waterfalls of blood
That bathe them nestled lying together and
As you touch this channel you are dislodging jewels,

Rubies pearls and diamonds, as each drops another forms, just as
I reached within you beginning at the
Moist cool anus and felt upward until my whole arm

Was enclosed and I felt your bowels
Your stomach your heart shaped elegantly like a pear
My hand cupped round continuing its labors

This was so nice would you drink anything warm
Offered foaming to you in a wooden bowl, by outstretched hands
The juices are harmless, they are not poison, they are life.

❧ Homecoming

We know that nothing
It says is true, necessarily. When the man
Returned, he was still attractive
And strong, after a decade of war and a decade
Of adventure, according to the story.

The wife floated his boat. She was a prize
Even as a young, slender girl, and
Was now a better one, richer, riper,
But he found this out only
After passing tests. First his dog recognized him,

Yap! Yap! then the stooped crone
Who had nursed him,
Then beautiful Penelope. He had to sneak
In, past a hundred swaggering
Male invaders.

Sullen they were, and arrogant, as snakes.
He frowned: rape artists.
Cold was his anger, and incredibly
Loosed was her burden of control at last.
From rock, she became water, and

In terror and tears,
Kill the sonofabitches! Kill them!
She said. And he did so,
He and the boy, together, in her honor,
Or the story says so.

A man is a fool who
Questions his weeping wife too curiously
(While the carcasses pile up) and a woman is a fool
Who thinks this life
Can ever offer safety,

My husband says that, and he happens to be
The man who wrote the brutal but idealistic
Iliad, while I am the woman who wrote
The romantic, domestic *Odyssey,* filled
With goddesses, mortal women, pigs, and homecoming.

The Impulse of Singing

—for Cid Corman

That journey he made
Because of an intolerable wound
That would not heal on earth, that he willed to heal

Although all called him fool, that journey
Down from song, down to the impulse of singing,
The pure kingdom of hell:

That was a famous visit
And a triumph. He descended. It seemed they melted,
Pitying. But ascending, he could not carry, hurl, rob

His bride back, and *this,* after all, was his object.
Can you image how he sang after that?
How bitterly beautiful, before the madwomen ripped him?

Excerpt from "Message from the Sleeper at Hell's Mouth"

Psyche Replies

> This, said Cupid, was the danger of which I warned you
> again and again. . . . But your punishment will simply be
> that I'll fly away from you.
> —*Apuleius*

It wasn't only my sisters
Making me want to see you,
Burn you, after the touching, the tidal kisses.

I knew you would be lovely,
A lane of flowering trees in a man's form, an army,
A ship of silks, fleeing me in hatred,

The scorch mark marring you.
I knew that I would weep, rise and get dressed,
And hunt you through the world.

Whatever happened, I said
Yes, and discovered that every
Time I said it I could

See further, more completely.
Yes, I said to my sisters,
It is you my husband wants,

You go leap off that cliff:
For they twisted their hands like worms
Upturned into a light that hurt.

Performing my tasks, one
After the other, I could see the desire
Of the ants, the reeds,

The tower itself to help me,
As if they were my music, I their voice.
I could see your mother's cruelty

Through her red smile, in heaven, where she lives,
Where I am going to live.
When her malice sent me to hell

The swarming dead implored me for a single
Touch, a single kiss.
No, I said.

In the last part of my story I saw pure
Evil, a hard bejeweled box of beauty.
It made me sleep awhile and dream.

The place behind my ribs became
More restful, like children
Settling down for an all-night game

Of cards or Monopoly
On a screened porch, a summer evening,
The moths and June bugs in a way

Included, but no bother.
Was it myself, then, in this dream, creeping
Up the wire mesh?

Anyway, what is the soul
But a dream of itself? it pictures
A girl pursuing a god

Who is lovely, naked, wounded,
And in her sleep she says
Come soon, friend, with your arrows.

❧ The Runner

—for Muriel Rukeyser

Sweat glides on the forehead of the gasping runner
Who runs of necessity, who runs possibly for love,
For truth, for death, and her feet are sweltering.

Behind the runner lies a battlefield.
There, the dust falls. Ahead, the narrow road
Eats a plateau, leads into streets and buildings,

A beach, and the excavation of motherly ocean,
Everything under the arch of an innocent sky.
Sweat trickles between her breasts, evaporates,

And the runner, seeing bright bone under brown landscape
Where one of us would see rocks, bushes, houses,
Begins to feel how fire invades a body

From within, first the splinters
And crumpled paper, then the middle wood
And the great damp logs splendidly catching.

Ah, but some moments! it is so like fireworks,
Hissing, exploding, flaring in darkness,
Or like a long kiss that she cannot stop,

And it is heavy for her, every stride
Like pulling an iron railing
Uphill, ah Christ—we would have to imagine Jerusalem,

Dresden, a hurt this hard, like a screen of fire
Rising, continuous and intolerable
Until solid things melt. Then the runner is floating,

She becomes herself a torch, she is writing in fire
Rejoice, we have triumphed, rejoice,
We have triumphed,

Although words, although language
Must be useless
To the runner.

A Minor Van Gogh (He Speaks):

The strokes are pulses: from my shapely cloud
And sky descending to distant hills
And closer hills, there is a far white tower
That rests, and in the foreground a muddy earth
Of ochre and purple strips, here is my soft clay, my
Bushy juicy green in the corner
And my plowman whom I make at
Dawn forever following his horse
Down the middle of the world. The strokes
Rush forward, waving their hats, identical,
All elements alike, all particles
Of Christ's material dancing, even
The shadowed furrow saying *I exist, I live!*
I also live, and make this form of Christ,
Locked in the light of earth, compassionate.

—"Landscape with Plowman," Fogg Museum

❧ Waterlilies and Japanese Bridge

He is the drowsy girl who rows "between the sleeping
Vegetations," Mallarmé calls them, "of an ever
Narrow and wandering stream," and he is a sage who drinks
Milk from the breasts of *le bon dieu* himself.

Like every artist, he is good and happy.
Bourgeois as possible, *mes petits,* like a bee.
Regular hours for mealtimes, slumber,
Labor in the poppy-beds, and moreover,
When a man earns three
Or four thousand francs a canvas, then he may
Whimper at some failing weather, or some broken flower.

May slash imperfect canvases, may pile them in a corner
Of garden and burn them, hooting. Like a porcupine, he
Snuffles and roots in the rosebushes, trots
Through the thin bamboo forest, comes to stand at the pond.
Green, and again green, and again
Mysterious lilies speechless on the water,
Pampas grass, willows, poplars, blocking sky.

Regular hours that are to eternity
As bootlace is to boot. Today he is painting
The overpainted bridge.
Penetrate, penetrate.
It is spots, curves, masses,
It is protected heat, it is his Africa and Asia
In a saucer, in a cupboard. It is admirable,
Like a wife's pregnant belly and a miser's sums.

This is the year he paints the bridge ten times,
Glutton of light, white butterfly among the green and white,
The pink and white, the deep sienna accents.
In nineteen twenty-two the cataracts
Will crawl, a fungus, over his lenses, he will paint red

Mud and whiplashes, and after this, he will fly out
Of himself among the swift canoeing molecules,
The waterlilies bursting like painless bombs
—Is it from him? or around him? His old man's forehead
Garlanded.

> —Claude Monet, "Waterlilies and Japanese Bridge," 1899,
> Princeton Art Museum

The Singing School

First they asked you to step through the many rooms
Until you came to the one where Father waited
Wearing his old chinos and sneakers.
It was painted eggshell. Two cups of coffee stood
On a rosewood table, and the night air blew
Pleasantly in at a half-open door.

He told you about his journey through a tunnel,
Saying that he was frightened.
Only he winked at you and laughed
About it while he talked.

Another time they set you in a blizzard
And you were wearing layers of heavy clothing.
With each removal of clothing the snow lessened.
Then finally you were naked, an August sun
Caressing you, and dragonflies were gliding
Above an oval pond . . .

Now you know how to sing.
Now you have to make
Your own story.

The Imaginary Lover

(1986)

❧ Cows

Dawn breaks
Blue and silver. You struggle against the hangover,
You fight the brutal cold, ice in the ruts.

You have thrown on your black cracked leather jacket
With the Grateful Dead button on the collar,
That you never even think of any more,

To go and breathe the sweet-sour
Gelatinous spoony brew
Emanating around them, filling up

The forty year old barn that was your father's.
Shivering, you curse them, but when all else shrinks,
Money, friends, women,

These unimpulsive bony forms remain
Gigantic as they ever were, echo
After droning echo, shadow after swaying shadow,

Brown and meaty. Like children they lock you
To the land, and all your life
While you lie asleep the flat of your hands

Will rehearse the feel
Of these beasts, or their daughters.
When you lean daily against their heat

And yank-and-pull,
As the milk in its balloons comes down
Pissing into the pail,

You also will sigh and swell,
Halfway between the past and future,
And rub your face, the way you did

When you were twelve and half afraid
Of either milk or sperm
Or blood, but guessed

Ahead to the good, as your father knew you would.

❧ Horses

—for Jana and Maxine

What was the first animal
People recognized as beautiful?

Not horses, probably the deer
And bison they hunted and painted

On the dry cave walls
During the long prehistorical afternoons.

But for us it is horses, in herds
And in themselves, vehement and glossy.

Their perspiration, their sleek ripples
Under the hide, their speed.

"Glorious as a horse," you might want to say.
Would you dive into the globular fierce jelly

Of a horse eye?
Solid barn of a body, needle legs—

Taste them in action, how we love horses
Cantering under our crotches, the hard

Facts of a landscape
Changing, blurring—

How we are glad to sail forward, to press
Undulant form with our knees, how we remember

Our parents, their whiskered nostrils, those sharp
Tunnels into eternity, and even

Now when they stop, bent
To our oated hands, muzzles so soft, the horses

Are never tamed, never entirely tamed.

❦ Staring at the Pacific, and Swimming in It

The mind, she thinks,
She meditates, she thinks

It feels out, it feels out all along
The thinking

Like fingers reaching
Into a glove

Feeling into the
Soft leather fingers

While the other hand pulls, or
Like running down to the warm

Beach, like diving into the
Surf and swimming

With all one's slick energy
Outward, outward

Though the water surges
Inward and outward

According to its own
Mysterious laws, which one

Senses yet disregards,
Feeling occasionally

The brush of some seaweed
Swaying, or a thwack

Of kelp, or a light fish kiss,
Pulling along

The intense red track, constantly moving
Of the sinking sun—what

Pleasure! What danger!
One is then beyond California!

Look around, see how the beach has dwindled,
Lost in

Haze, how the ocean holds.

❦ Three Men Walking, Three Brown Silhouettes

They remember the dead who died in the resistance.
It is in sweet tones that they speak of them.
They shake their heads, still, after the dinner

Walking back to the car, while an evening snow
That has started windlessly, white from pearl-gray,
Falls into streets that are already slushy.

They shake their heads, as we do when there is something
Too strange to believe,
Or as a beast does, stunned by a blow.

"To die in the resistance," they say, "is to fail
To turn into slush, to escape this ugliness.
It is at once to leap, a creamy swan,

Upward." Three voices: oboe, piano, cello.
The high one wishes to be pleasing, the middle
To be practical, the deep to persevere.

A movie theater lobby in front of them
Throws its light on the sidewalk, like a woman
Swiftly emptying a bucket of water:

The flakes are falling in its yellow light.
Then they pass a café, its light red neon,
Then a closed pharmacy.

                              —They pull sharp air
Into their lungs, a pain that is a pleasure.
"Try to live as if there were no God,"
They don't say, but they mean.

A recollection of purity, a clean
Handkerchief each man feels in his own pocket,
Perturbs them, slows their pace down. Now they have seen

A yellow stain on a pile of old snow
Between two parked cars, where a man has peed:
The resistance. The falling flakes, falling

On the men's hats. And now
The snow grows heavier, falls on their stooping shoulders.

❧ Mother in Airport Parking Lot

This motherhood business fades, is almost over.
I begin to reckon its half-life.
I count its tears, its expended tissues,

And I remember everything, I remember
I swallowed the egg whole, the oval
Smooth and delicately trembling, a firm virgin

Sucked into my oral chamber
Surrendered to my mouth, my mouth to it.
I recall how the interior gold burst forth

Under pressure, secret, secret,
A pleasure softer, crazier than orgasm.
Liquid yolk spurted on my chin,

Keats's grape, and I too a trophy,
I too a being in a trance,
The possession of a goddess.

Multiply the egg by a thousand, a billion.
Make the egg a continuous egg through time,
The specific time between the wailing birth cry

And the child's hand wave
Accompanied by thrown kiss at the airport.
Outside those brackets, outside my eggshell, and running

Through the parking lot in these very balmy
September breezes—what? And who am I?
The world is flat and happy,

I am in love with asphalt
So hot you could fry an egg on it,
I am in love with acres of automobiles,

None of them having any messy feelings.
Here comes a big bird low overhead,
A tremendous steel belly hurtles over me,

Is gone, pure sex, and I love it.
I am one small woman in a great space,
Temporarily free and clear.

I am by myself, climbing into my car.

ॐ The Marriage Nocturne

Stopped at a corner, near midnight, I watch
A young man and young woman quarreling
Under the streetlamp. What I can see is gestures.
He leans forward, he scowls, raises his hand.
She has been taking it, but now she stands
Up to him, throwing her chin and chest out.
The stoplight purples their two leather jackets.
Both of them now are shouting, theatrical,
Shut up, bitch, or, Go to hell, loser,
And between them, in a stroller,
Sits their pale bundled baby, a piece of candy.

Earlier this evening I was listening
To the poet Amichai, whose language seemed
To grow like Jonah's gourd in a dry place,
From pure humility, or perhaps from yearning
For another world, land, city
Of Jerusalem, while embracing this one,
As a man dreams of the never-obtainable mistress,
Flowery, perfumed, girlish
(But hasn't she somehow been promised to him?)
And meanwhile has and holds the stony wife
Whom the Lord gives him for a long reproach.

I can imagine, when such a husband touches
Such a wife, hating it, in tears,
And helpless lust, and the survivor's shame,
That her eyes gaze back at him like walls
Where you still can see the marks of the shelling.

We make beauty of bitterness. Woman and man,
Arab and Jew, we have arrived at that
Dubious skill. Still, when one of these two,
Having moved like a dancer, smashes the other
One in the face, and the baby swivels its periscope

Neck to look, I will not see it:
The light changes. Fifteen miles down the road,
That will be lined by luminous spring trees,
My husband reads in bed, sleepy and naked;
I am not crying, I step on the gas, I am driving
Home to my marriage, my safety, through this wounded
World that we cannot heal, that is our bride.

🪶 Surviving

> Soon the time will come when I don't have to be ashamed
> and keep quiet but feel with pride that I am a painter.
>
> —*Paula Modersohn-Becker to her mother, July 1902*

i

It is true that in this century
To survive is to be ashamed.
We want to lie down in the unmarked grave,
We want to feel the policeman's club that cracks
A person's head like a honey-melon, and lets
Human life spill like seeds, we want to go up
In milky smoke like a promise.
If we're women it's worse, the lost ones
Leach our strength even when we are dancing,
Crying *no right* under our shoes.
When we are working, there is that nameless weariness:
Lie down, lie down, a mule in a dusty ditch
The cart shattered into boards—
Who can urge us to pull ourselves onward?
How can the broken mothers teach us?

It is true that when I encounter another
Story of a woman artist, a woman thinker
Who died in childbirth, I want to topple over
Sobbing, tearing my clothing.

ii

A painting of a peasant woman's hands
As strong as planks, influenced by Cézanne
Who had struck her "like a thunderstorm, a great event,"
That first visit from Germany to Paris.
She was a raw girl, then,
But the thought was clear.
A coarse canvas of an orange, a lemon,
Local deep-red tomatoes, two Fauve asters,
Globes and rays,

Designed like a reclining cross.
A naked woman and baby painted curled
On a mat, lacking a blanket, a portrait
Of what all skin remembers
And forgets.

I walked from painting to painting, I watched this woman's
Earth pigments growing thicker, more free,
More experimental,
Force augmented, it seemed, every year.
"The strength with which a subject
Is grasped, that's the beauty of art"
She wrote in her diary.
And she had resisted the marriage to Otto,
Had wished to remain in Paris
Painting like a Parisian, a modernist
But he had begged.
When they returned home, she knew herself
Already pregnant, delighted with pregnancy.

iii

(1876–1907)
The little cards on the gallery wall
Explained the story.
Language is a form of malice.
Language declares: *Here is a dead thing.*
I cover it over with my thin blanket.
And here is another dead thing.
Please to notice, you soon can feel
Nothing. Not true. I could feel the heart
Attack, as she rose from childbed, the beleaguered
Grief in my chest and womb,
That throttled cry, nature is not our enemy,
Or the enemy is also the ally,
The father, the mother,
The powerful helpless hills
Where the pigment comes from.

iv

Only the paintings were not elegiac.
The paintings, survivors
Without malice—can it be?
Squeezed into me like a crowd
Into an elevator
At nine A.M. Pressing against each other,
carrying their briefcases in one hand,
Pushing my buttons with the other,
Go ahead up, they said,
You have no choice.
Carry us to our floors, our destinations,
Smoothly if you will, do not break down.
On the first floor
When the doors slid open
A child rested her chin on a city stoop
Among the giants.
There were many such scenes, viewed briefly.
At the forty-sixth floor, before
The doors could close, my mother
Rushed inside, carrying her shopping bags
And wearing her scuffed loafers.
Alone in the elevator
At the mercy of the elevator
So much space around her,
Four planes of polished aluminum,
Such indirect lighting,
Such clean and grinning chrome.
An entire blankness
And she was trusting it
To bear her down,
And she was talking, talking.

v

Today I got a big bargain
In chickens, she says, and a pretty big bargain
In skim milk. Skim milk's bluish

Like mother's milk. Did I ever tell you
I fought the doctors and nurses
The very day you were born. They said
"You'll stick a bottle in her mouth"
But I nursed you, I showed
Them. And did I tell you
When I was hungry because your father
Didn't have a job, I used to feed you
That expensive beef puree, spoonful by spoonful,
Until you would throw up,
And then I would feed you a certain amount
More to make sure you were full
Although I was starving.
Did I tell you that one.

Mother, a hundred times.

Did I tell you I was president
Of the literary society
When your father met me.
Did I say that he called me "Beatrice
Of the beautiful eyes."
Did I tell you about the prize
I won for my poems.

Yes.

The checkout girl at the Shoprite
Tried to cheat me
Today but I caught her.
I told George but he was watching television.
He never pays attention, he pretends
He's deaf. Would you phone me
Saturday.

vi

So my mother should have been a writer. Her mother,
A Russian beauty, should have been a singer.

"She lost the bloom of her youth in the factories,"
My mother says, a formula sentence she is obviously
Repeating, and her eyes fill up like paper cups.
It is seventy years later. Explain these tears.

No promise of help or safety, every promise of cruelty,
Impoverishment, that is our world. John Keats loved it,
Coughing bright red. Hart Crane, also, sank into it,
Like a penny the veal-white passenger throws
Into the water to watch the boys who will
Dive. Explain *St. Agnes' Eve*. Explain *The Bridge*.

Explain these tears.

vii

We are running and skipping the blocks
To the Thomas Jefferson swimming pool
Where we'll both get in free
For the morning session,
You pretending to be my under-twelve
Elf-faced sister, and when we've gone through
The echoing cavernous locker room
Where underfed young Irish girls shiver
Knock-kneed as skeletons, the water drops
Standing out on their skin like blisters,
And we're in the water
Green and chlorinous
Cool in the August day
You hug me, mother, and we play
Diving under each other's legs
Until children collect around you like minnows
And you lead us in ring-a-rosy,
You get even the smallest ones to duck
Heads underwater, bubbling and giggling
Don't be afraid! Breathe out like this! Then we all sing
Songs against Hitler and the Japs.
I get to be closest. You're mine, I'm good.

We climb out, dripping on the tiles—
That bright day's faded. Today you are still running
As if you pushed a baby carriage
From a burning neighborhood.

viii

What woman doesn't die in childbirth
What child doesn't murder the mother
The stories are maps to nowhere

ix

A late self-portrait: it's a screen of foliage green
Enough to be purple, and here in front of it
The woman artist, crude, nude to the waist,
Fingers her amber beads, secretly
Smiling, like no man's wife
But like a mother's grown
Daughter, thriving and free—

x

Mother my poet, tiny harmless lady
Sad white-headed one
With your squirrel eyes
Your pleading love-me eyes
I have always loved you
Always dreaded you
And now you are nearly a doll
A little wind-up toy
That marches in a crooked circle
Emitting vibrations and clicks.
Mother, if what is lost
Is lost, there remains the duty
Proper to the survivor.
I ask the noble dead to strengthen me.
Mother, chatterer, I ask you also,
You who poured Tennyson

And Browning into my child ear, and you
Who threw a boxful of papers, your novel,
Down the incinerator
When you moved, when your new husband
Said to take only
What was necessary, and you took
Stacks of magazines, jars
Of buttons, trunks of raggy
Clothing, but not your writing.
Were you ashamed? Don't
Run away, tell me my duty,
I will try not to be deaf—
Tell me it is not merely the duty of grief.

Los Angeles, 1977 / Princeton, 1985

❧ Meeting the Dead

If we've loved them, it's what we want, and sometimes
Wanting works. With my father it happened driving
From Santa Monica to Pasadena
A night of a full moon, the freeway wide
Open, the palm trees black. I was recalling
How for two years after that shy man's death
I thought only of death, how in April weather
I used to lock the Volkswagen window so nothing
Pleasant or fragrant would reach me, how one time
I saw him staring in a ladies' room
Mirror, and stood in my tracks, paralyzed,
He looked so bitter, until his face dissolved
Back into my face. . . . My radio was playing
The usual late night jazz. No other cars
Drove with me on the freeway. I hated it
That we would never meet in mutual old
Age to drink a beer—it was all he ever
Drank—and declare our love the way I'd planned
All through high school, picturing us in
A sunny doorway facing a back garden;
Something out of a book. I hated it
That I was pushing forty and could still
Curl like a snail, a fetus, weeping for him.
While I was feeling that, the next things happened
All at once, like iron slugs
Being pulled into a magnet.
This has been *mourning,* I thought; then a sound came,
Like a door clicking closed, and I understood
Right off that I was finished, that I would
Never feel any more misery for him—
And at the same time, he was present; had been,
I now saw, all along, for these twelve years,
Waiting for me to finish my mourning.
At that I had to laugh, and he swiftly slipped
From outside the Buick, where he had been floating.

I was still doing about sixty.
He was just in me. His round eyesockets
Were inside mine, his shoulderblades aligned
With my own, his right foot and right palm
Lay with mine on the gas pedal and steering wheel—
A treat for him who'd never learned to drive.
The San Gabriel foothills were approaching
Like parents, saying here's a friend for life,
And then they blocked the moon, and I was back
On suburb streets, I was quietly passing
The orderly gardens and homes of the living.

Los Angeles 1977 / Princeton 1985

✿ Listen

—for Rebecca

Having lost you, I attract substitutes.
The student poets visit, think me wise,
Think me generous, confide in me.
Earnestly they sit in my office
Showing me their stigmata
Under the Judy Chicago poster
Of her half-opened writhing-petalled
Clitoris that appears to wheel
Slowly clockwise when you gaze at it,
And I sympathize. Then they try on their ambitions
Like stiff new hiking boots, and I laugh
And approve, telling them where to climb.
They bring me tiny plastic bags
Of healthy seeds and nuts, they bring me wine,
We huddle by the electric heater
When it is snowing,
We watch the sparrows dash
And when they leave we hug.

Oh silly mother, I can hear you mock.
Listen, loveliest, I am not unaware
This is as it must be.
Do daughters mock their mothers? Is Paris
A city? Do your pouring hormones
Cause you to do the slam
And other Dionysiac dances,
And did not even Sappho tear her hair
And act undignified, when the maiden
She wanted, the girl with the soft lips,
The one who could dance,
Deserted her?

Do I suffer? Of course I do,
I am supposed to, but listen, loveliest.
I want to be a shrub, you a tree.
I hum inaudibly and want you
To sing arias. I want to lie down
At the foot of your mountain
And rub the two dimes in my pocket
Together, while you dispense treasure
To the needy. I want the gods
Who have eluded me
All my life, or whom I have eluded,
To invite you regularly
To their lunches and jazz recitals.
Moreover I wish to stand on the dock
All by myself waving a handkerchief,
And you to be the flagship
Sailing from the midnight harbor,
A blue moon leading you outward,
So huge, so public, so disappearing—

I beg and beg, loveliest, I can't
Seem to help myself,
While you quiver and pull
Back, and try to hide, try to be
Invisible, like a sensitive
Irritated sea animal
Caught in a tide pool, caught
Under my hand, can I
Cut off my hand for you,
Cut off my life.

A Question of Time

I ask a friend. She informs me it is ten years
From when her mother wrote
"I hope at least you are sorry
For causing your father's heart attack,"
To now, when they are speaking
Weekly on the phone
And almost, even, waxing confidential.
I check my watch. Ten years is rather much,
But I am not a Texas fundamentalist,
And you are not a red-headed lesbian,
So it should take us shorter, and I should get
Time off for good behavior
If I behave well, which
I do not plan to do.
No, on the contrary, I plan to play
All my cards wrong,
To pelt you with letters, gifts, advice,
Descriptions of my feelings.
I plan to ask friendly maternal questions.
I plan to beam a steady
Stream of anxiety
Rays which would stun a mule,
Derail a train,
Take out a satellite,
At you in California, where you hack
Coldly away at this iron umbilicus,
Having sensibly put three thousand miles between us.

I remember you told me once, when we were still
In love, the summer before you left
For the hills of San Francisco,
The music of youth,
To stop fearing estrangement:
"Mom, you're not crazy like grandma."
It was the country. We were on the balcony

Overlooking the pond, where your wiry boyfriend
And the rest of the family swam and drank, unconscious.
False but endearing, dear. I *am* my mother.
I am your mother. Are you keeping up
Your drawing, your reading?
Have you written poems?
Are you saving money? Don't
Do acid, it fries the brain,
Don't do cocaine, don't
Get pregnant, or have you already,
Don't slip away from me,
You said you wouldn't,
Remember that. I remember it was hot,
How lightly we were dressed,
And barefoot, at that time,
And how you let me rest
A half a minute in your suntanned arms.

Years

—for J.P.O.

I have wished you dead and myself dead,
How could it be otherwise.
I have broken into you like a burglar
And you've set your dogs on me.
You have been a hurricane to me
And a pile of broken sticks
A child could kick.
I have climbed you like a monument, gasping,
For the exercise and the view,
And leaned over the railing at the top—
Strong and warm, that summer wind.

❧ I Brood About Some Concepts, for Example

A concept like "I," which I am told by many
Intellectual experts has no

Signification outside of language.
I don't believe that, do you? Of course not.

If I kick myself, do I not
Hurt my foot, and if I fuck

A friend, or even if I masturbate,
Do I not come? Somebody does,

I think it's me, I like to call her "me,"
And I assume you like to call the one

Who comes (it is sweet, isn't it,
While birth and death are bitter, we figure,

But sexuality, in the middle there, is so
Sweet!) when you come, "me" and "I" also,

No harm in that, in fact considerable
Justice I feel, and don't you also feel?

Coito ergo
Sum, you remark. Good, so that settles it

With or without the words . . .
Meanwhile the errant philosopher

Whatshisname, the eminent Marxist/Lacanian
Linguist, the very lettered one,

Whose penis leaks
Alphabets, the poor creature, perhaps

Doesn't come at all, doesn't
Like cakes and ale, really

Can't taste them, doesn't
Feel pain and pleasure, is afraid to

Touch himself, or admit it—oh, it is
Turning white all around him,

Look at it turning white all around him
Like a special effect in a film,

A kind of confetti blizzard—he won't admit it—
Frowning, tapping, I assume he is a man,

The keys, the dry air
Filling up with signs around him,

Rather frightening, white and whispering, and faintly
Buzzing, the colors draining

Gradually from him
And the rectangles of windowpane—

Oh, this is
Shocking, an X ray flash a sort of

Twenties black and white, the scholar
A skeleton! The skull grinning

As skulls do! Merely a flash,
But yes, I am convinced there is no

"I" there, I assume I am seeing language,
So that is what he intended, they intended

To disclose. The thing itself . . .

Taking the Shuttle with Franz

A search for metaphors to describe the thick
Pork faces and large torsos of businessmen.
I am encountering a fiendish wall
Of these on the Newark-Boston 9:35 shuttle flight.
My friend Franz Kafka has his nose in a book,
As ever, preparing his lecture notes, while I
Weave among the strangers, spindling and unspindling
My boarding pass, and am aghast with admiration for the cut
Of their suits, the fineness of their shirt
Fabrics, and the deep gloss of their shoe leather.

But what amazes me most is the vast expanse
Of clothing required fully to cover them,
So that one fancies a little mustached tailor
Unrolling hopefully bolt after bolt of excellent
Woolen stuff. How lucky they are, after all,
That stores sell jackets, trousers, etcetera,
In these palatial sizes.
What if they had to clothe their nakedness
With garments made for lesser men?
It would have to be in patches, possibly

Even with stretches of raw flesh showing.
As it is, they look good
Enough to ski on. And they talk
In firm but thoughtful voices, about money.
Only about money. It is not my aural delusion.
It is commodities, it is securities.
"Franz," I whisper, "take a look. What do you think?"
Of course I cannot consider them human, any
More than I would consider the marble columns
Of an Attic temple human. Franz agrees,

But sees them more as resembling something Chinese,
Perhaps the Great Wall. Similarly, they,

Although they speak of money,
Glance at from their eye pouches at us, low
Of stature, ineffably shabby (we
Have dressed our best), with "Intellectual"
Scripted messily in ballpoint across our foreheads.
Now as they do so, the athletic heart
Throbs within them, under cashmere and cambric:
"Vermin," they think, imagining stamping us out.

Everywoman Her Own Theology

I am nailing them up to the cathedral door
Like Martin Luther. Actually, no,
I don't want to resemble that *Schmutzkopf*
(See Erik Erikson and N. O. Brown
On the Reformer's anal aberrations,
Not to mention his hatred of Jews and peasants),
So I am thumbtacking these ninety-five
Theses to the bulletin board in my kitchen.

My proposals, or should I say requirements,
Include at least one image of a god,
Virile, beard optional, one of a goddess,
Nubile, breast size approximating mine,
One divine baby, one lion, one lamb,
All nude as figs, all dancing wildly,
All shining. Reproducible
In marble, metal, in fact any material.

Ethically, I am looking for
An absolute endorsement of loving-kindness.
No loopholes except maybe mosquitoes.
Virtue and sin will henceforth be discouraged,
Along with suffering and martyrdom.
There will be no concept of infidels.
Consequently the faithful must entertain
Themselves some other way than killing infidels.

And so forth and so on. I understand
This piece of paper is going to be
Spattered with wine one night at a party
And covered over with newer pieces of paper.
That is how it goes with bulletin boards.
Nevertheless it will be there.
Like an invitation, like a chalk pentangle,
It will emanate certain occult vibrations.

If something sacred wants to swoop from the universe
Through a ceiling, and materialize,
Folding its silver wings,
In a kitchen, and bump its chest against mine,
My paper will tell this being where to find me.

Poem Beginning with a Line by Fitzgerald/Hemingway

The very rich are different from us, they
Have more money, fewer scruples. The very

Attractive have more lovers, the very sensitive
Go mad more easily, and the very brave

Distress a coward like myself, so listen
Scott, listen Ernest, and you also can

Listen, Walt Whitman. I understand the large
Language of rhetoricians, but not the large

Hearts of the heroes. I am reading up.
I want someone to tell me what solvent saves

Their cardiac chambers from sediment, what is
The shovel that cuts the sluice

Straight from the obvious mottoes such as *Love*
Your neighbor as yourself, or *I am human, therefore*

Nothing human is alien, to the physical arm
In the immaculate ambassadorial shirtsleeves

—We are in Budapest, '44—that waves
Off the muddy Gestapo in the railroad yard

With an imperious, an impatient flourish,
And is handing Swedish passports to anonymous

Yellow-starred arms reaching from the very boxcars
That are packed and ready to glide with a shrill

Whistle and grate on steel, out of the town,
Like God's biceps and triceps gesturing

Across the void to Adam: Live. In Cracow
A drinking, wenching German businessman

Bribes and cajoles, laughs and negotiates
Over the workers, spends several times a fortune,

Saves a few thousand Jews, including one
He wins at a card game, and sets to work

In his kitchenware factory. A summer twilight
Soaks a plateau in southern France, the mountains

Mildly visible, and beyond them Switzerland,
As the policeman climbs from the khaki bus

To Le Chambon square, where the tall pastor
Refuses to give names of refugees;

Meanwhile young men slip through the plotted streets,
Fan out to the farms—it is '42—

So that the houses empty and the cool woods fill
With Jews and their false papers, so that the morning

Search finds no soul to arrest. It happens
Over and over, but how? The handsome Swede

Was rich, was bored, one might have said. The pastor
Had his habit of hugging and kissing, and was good

At organizing peasants, intellectuals
And bible students. The profiteer intended

To amass wealth. He did, lived steep, and ended
Penniless, though the day the war ended,

The day they heard, over the whistling wireless,
the distant voice of Churchill barking victory

As the Russians advanced, his *Schindlerjuden*
Still in the plant, still safe, as he moved to flee,

Made him a small present. Jerets provided
His mouth's gold bridgework, Licht melted it down,

Engraved the circle of the ring with what
One reads in Talmud: *Who saves a single life,*

It is as if he saved the universe; and Schindler
The German took it, he wears it in his grave;

I am reading up on this. I did not know
Life had undone so many deaths. *Now go*

And do likewise, snaps every repercussion
Of my embarrassed heart, which is like a child

Alone in a classroom full of strangers, thinking
She would like to run away. Let me repeat,

Though I do not forget ovens or guns,
Their names: Raoul Wallenberg, Oskar Schindler,

André Trocmé. Europe was full of others
As empty space is full of burning suns;

Not equally massive or luminous,
Creating heat, nevertheless, and light,

Creating what we may plausibly write
Up as the sky, a that without which nothing;

We cannot guess how many, only that they
Were subject to arrest each bloody day

And managed. Maybe it's like the muse, incalculable,
What you can pray in private for. Or a man

You distantly adore, who may someday love you
In the very cave of loneliness. We are afraid—

Yet as no pregnant woman knows beforehand
If she will go through labor strong, undrugged,

Unscreaming, and no shivering soldier knows
During pre-combat terror who will retreat,

Who stand and fight, so we cannot predict
Who among us will risk the fat that clings

Sweetly to our own bones—
None sweeter, Whitman promises—

Our life, to save doomed lives, and none of us
Can know before the very day arrives.

🙞 The War of Men and Women

He has come for help,
A talented young man, a poet
Whom I love
But I am not helping.

i

I write in rage against my sex—
What else am I to do? Friend, if your frightened woman
Won't come across, because she's pretty strong, because
She has the whip hand over you, because her mother
And her mother's mother told her: *Use this power,*
Honey, it's all you got, you better make
Them somersault and juggle, make them beg, calculate
Every move, or they'll brutalize you, utilize you, take
What you can, sweetheart, give nothing you don't have to—

They did not need to say those things in words,
The ghost grandmothers,
The manipulators,
The same idea rose from the mirror,
The trousseau, the dowry,
The laws of property,
The entrance into the village
Of the army.

Good girls and bad girls, virgins and prostitutes,
Angels in the house and bitches
In the bed, those are our veils, our masks, and behind them
Are fools and smart women, don't forget it,
Crooned the crone arranging the maiden's hair,
The flushed woman slapping her daughter's face
At the first blood, the bones of the dead sister
In the churchyard beside her newborn,
Whining into the ears
Of the sweating survivors.

One might have said, *if you give the milk away*
For free, nobody will buy the cow. Another
Would be praying for her daughter's purity
While ironing. Having broken the chicken's neck,
Another would play with the handle
Of her great kitchen knife—

I write in rage against your sex, although
Here you sit in my kitchen, sipping
My Earl Grey, face perplexed, the sighing victim
Who never reads jock novelists, who never
Leafs through a *Playboy* in the airport bookstore,
Who has not seen *Deep Throat,* the gentle knight
Whose hanging sword is mocked, whose fathers
Burned out their lives like casual cigarettes
That yellow a man's fingers,
In the office, the shop, the assembly lines, the mines,
And never wanted
Anything but a little female comfort.

ii

Contents of one day's mail. Amnesty International
Reports on Chilean tortures, new methods
You don't want to know about.

There is a description of what
They do to dissidents in Soviet
Psychiatric hospitals, you don't want to know about.

My friend writes, the Colorado man
Was convicted of murdering his wife
For what he called deceiving him. She promised

She wouldn't run away after he beat her
Then she did run away, so he found her and shot her
And has been sentenced to two years in prison.

By the way, while you are getting angry
When policemen kill black people
They are acquitted

Or never brought to trial.

I read your mind: you are wondering
What kind of people could
What kind of monsters

Do you know, my innocent friend
As I pour you a cup of tea
Sometimes I want to kill you.

iii
Please, you say
Help me, I can't think
About anything with my marriage
Up in the air like this
Somehow I can't please her
I am just living from day to day
I can't get my work done

Is she seeing somebody
Else, you say, does she
Need a vacation, one drink and she starts
In on me, sneering, we can't afford a bigger
Apartment, she used to want me.

iv
The State of the Union:
In 1973 the "Liberty Oak"
At the battlefield monument

Said to have been a sapling
At the time of the Revolution
Now strung together with cables

But still majestic looking
Master of all it surveyed
Was struck by lightning

Lost one third of its crown
Survives but is
Not beautiful to look at.

v

Forgive me
      You are crying
            I like to see men cry

vi

I run my mind over a handful of names
That lie lightly in the palm as a cone of sand,
William Lloyd Garrison, Frederick Douglas, Ibsen. . . .
The merely clear, the merely rational
Human insight; or Lincoln's *As I would not*
Be a slave, so I would not be a master. . . .
I look at my fingers, stubby, the nails uneven,
Sands run between my fingers
And the mountainrange names remain, the unchanging
Sculpted faces:
Moses, Plato, Saul of Tarsus, Alp
After lofty Alp, spectacular, and not one
Who desires my life and freedom as his own.

I get tired, don't you,
Of being a miner, crawling around, coughing,
Hacking at dead rock, far from the mountain air,
Of being the boatload
Of refugees raped and throat-slit by pirates,
Of being the drooling infant
In time of famine,
Of being the doctor who explains
Diagnosis is easy, cure impossible.

Every mechanical failure,
From your wife's coldness, your limpness, your child's
Stupidities in school, to these matters
Of human sewage touched on in the mail,
My nation feeding death to the wide world,
My vision of the president's pink
Tongue lapping red blood up—
Every one is the failure of the imagination, the failure
To join our life with the dangerous life of the other,
And we would need an archaeology
Of pain to trace the course of this frozen river.

I get tired of this pulpy body.
I get damned tired of telling people
What they already know.

vii

Sometimes you feel on the border: an ounce more effort
Will hurl you into the state of enlightenment.
Your ego will fall apart like the charmed chains
That bound the burning hero until he woke.

You try to recall the rapture of love,
How easy it was to be generous then,
A thread in a vast weft, and the picture
Complete and clear, the millefleurs

And the architecture, the beasts,
The hunters and strolling couples, the zodiac
Framing the edges, yourself believing
Nothing too difficult, and when the ladder

Of soft kisses scaled higher, you leaned like the figure
In the ancient brass astrolabe who pierces
The bowl of our capricious sky and gazes
At last at the true Cosmos.

Everyone who has been in eternity knows
It is not discipline
It is sudden surrender
Merely the fallen walls, the blue, the breeze,
The stairs to the water
And you can nearly smell what you desire

But every minute your pain is worse.

You feel as if you are choking
Or giving birth.
It is like the door in your dream
That you knocked at,
Pressed your face against, kicked,
And finally understood
That it would never open.

               And I didn't

Ask you to touch me.
Man, stay away,
Eat your cookie, drink your tea.
You falsely think I mean to comfort you.

viii

Heaps of broken stones weathering slowly, a mountain
May break by jointing, cracking, spalling, slabbing.
Sandstone breaks into slabs or plates, schist
Into splintery pieces, cleavages become zones
Of weakness, cracks form among them.
At times severe jointing in massive rocks spontaneously
Occurs when they open tunnels far underground, releasing
Previous pressure on the rocks in those passageways

        So to dig and carry up material
        May release the mass somewhat
        While the worker is the more endangered

Once the cracks are present, water, bacteria and plant roots
Enlarge and wedge the fissure apart. Sedimentary limestone,
Formed from the shells of armored animals, goes
Quickly, they say, in temperate climates.

To pass the fingertip over the silver vein
In the feldspar as the rains begin: will the rock crack,
How much of it will fragment this season,
What will the rootlets, the floods
The swarming nations of bacteria
Accomplish this year, or this century?

Sometimes we wish, O God, the simple blast
That would blow our fossil selves to smithereens,
Cough up the melt, the ash, the inner
Foulness. . . .

It is late in the afternoon.
The white mouse in the laboratory maze
Runs, changes direction, twitches his whiskers,
His intelligence races,
A yellow bar of sunlight, in which gray motes
Are flying, touches his cage.

ix

The worst of it is that we hear the dead
Continually beseeching us
In their reedy voices, droning

Below their other messages, more blind,
More insistent, telling us
To heal ourselves.

Please, they beg, and explain
They depend on us
As all parents depend upon all children.

The dead are in my kitchen
Among the scattered crumbs, the tea-leaves,
The amber tea we have almost finished,

The paper napkins we have twisted and shredded.
They wonder if they can help tidy up.
They glance hopefully from my face to your face.

You can't get there from here, said the Vermont farmer
To the city people who asked directions.

Try it?
Take one step to repair your own damage?

I too want to be healed
By some other person, some wise being, some saint
And there is no saint

There is my crippled self, who wipes the crumbs
Into a garbage bag,
Hands you your jacket back, lets

You go home.

A Clearing by a Stream

What impels the mind to soar forth?
What makes breath start?
What causes people to speak?
Eye and ear—what god is making them live?

    Gabriel, when we were camping, saw a deer—
        From what does not perish emerges what perishes—

A pale violet butterfly stops near me.
When its wings are closed I cannot see the color.
When it opens its wings and flies my eyes cannot

Follow its speedy fluttering trajectory.
How then can we expect to satisfy
Our hearts with seeing?

Now it's flown off, as I anticipated,
Over the stream a minute, and now has settled
Next to me again, with my sketchbook and pen.

It opens its wings partially.
Staring, I see the pink and blue pigments
Mixing on them, very faintly shimmering,

And the thin brown veins.
Each wing having two petals,
It writhes them,

Independently,
Sensually, unlike
What I expected of a butterfly.

It stands with wings half-open in thought;
Wind pushes them. Its body is solid
Violet, long and hairy, like velveteen.

Again it loops away. Do the weeds and flowers
Take it for another flower, strangely able
To float and alight? Look at that one,

They whisper, it is stemless
And rootless! Is the butterfly to the plant
As the Great Self to ourselves?

It's back. I rest my forefinger
Next to it, and it isn't afraid, it mounts
My ridged finger and walks stiffly across my hand.

Letting the Doves Out

The imaginary lover, form in the mind
On whom, as on a screen, I project designs,
Images, whose presence makes me dilate

Until I become a flock of puffy doves
Cooing and cooing in a magician's hat, my pigeonblood-
Ruby hearts beating, pure wings set for flight,

For dispersion above the astonished audience
That sits applauding in the auditorium,
Wonderful, while the doves spiral and settle

Back in the brooding hat, tucked muffins,
White contours begging caressing thumbs, the thready
Magenta entrails packed inside each one:

What's his connection with you, oh playful stranger
With whom I have danced drunkenly,
Thinking "The more I dance, the more I want to,"

Eaten the elongated lunch or two,
Talked films, books, carelessly brushed the hand
That carelessly brushed mine, spelling "pretend,

Would you," and for how long can we sustain
These illusions, like magicians' scarves tossed in the air?
How long can even imaginary scarves

Continue to float, to bell out like sails
On a rough lake,
To twirl in the airy theatre

Colorfully, painlessly
As the silks in India,
To create a picture of love and liberty?

We ought to leave these matters to our haughty
Daughters, our humorous sons.
Having dreamed so for decades, since the first

Tall gamy lad flashed on that startled "inward
Eye . . . the bliss of solitude,"
I am half ashamed, but only half. The other

Half shameless, no, enchanted, imagines lovers:
Thunders, dry as I am, to invent storms,
To feel their needy pressure squeezing words

Out of my cave as if it were a hat,
My humming, murmuring and dewy cave
Cut in the living rock.

And what of you? You, the reality
Without whom my invention invents nothing?
Oh actual masculine, oh corduroy pants,

Oh imaginary lover, oh father-mother,
I want my liberty, my excitement,
My lullaby, wickedness and goodness,

Like the ensemble of sleepy musicians
Sawing and yawning in the auditorium's pit,
So long familiar they can improvise

A gaudy fanfare while the amused magician
Lets his doves out, murmurs them home again
And draws more iridescent scarves from his sleeve.

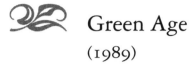 Green Age

(1989)

✿ Fifty

This is what a fifty-
Year-old woman looks like,
Said the glamorous feminist
Journalist when they asked her
How it felt to look so young.
A good answer.
But she didn't say, and they didn't
Ask her:
Did you expect the thread
Of your rough childhood
To unwind so far
From its beginnings?
Do you perhaps wonder,
When you try to look backward
And the thread seems invisible, as if
It has been snipped, who
In the world you are,
Stranger?
Do you think: *Let's keep this thing*
Rolling, keep on fighting, keep
Up the good work,
And glare down the steel tracks of the mirror
At the approach of the enemy
Who is still miles away
But coming like a commuter train, do you
Hit your typewriter
Every day, harder
And harder, like a recalcitrant
Spoiled child, have you surrendered
The hope of the perfect
Romance, or do you grip that
Fantasy stubbornly, like a kid holding

On to a dead pet
That she knows is dead
And do you make a joke of all of this
And when the clock says *Almost
Quitting time,* do you still answer *Never?*

A Young Woman, a Tree

i

The life spills over, some days.
She cannot be at rest,
Wishes she could explode

Like that red tree—
The one that bursts into fire
All this week.

Senses her infinite smallness
But can't seize it,
Recognizes the folly of desire,

The folly of withdrawal—
Kicks at the curb, the pavement,
If only she could, at this moment,

When what she's doing is plodding
To the bus stop, to go to school,
Passing that fiery tree—if only she could

Be making love,
Be making poetry,
Be exploding, be speeding through the universe

Like a photon, like a shower
Of yellow blazes—
She believes if she could only overtake

The riding rhythm of things, of her own electrons,
Then she would be at rest—
If she could forget school,

Climb the tree,
Be the tree,
Burn like that.

ii

She doesn't know yet, how could she,
That this same need
Is going to erupt every September

And that in forty years the idea will strike her
From no apparent source, in a laundromat
Between a washer and a dryer,

Like one of those electric light bulbs
Lighting up near a character's head in a comic strip—
There in that naked and soiled place

With its detergent machines,
Its speckled fluorescent lights,
Its lint piles broomed into corners,

As she fumbles for quarters
And dimes, she will start to chuckle and double over
Into the plastic basket's

Mountain of wet
Bedsheets and bulky overalls—
Old lady! She'll grin, beguiled at herself,

Old lady! The desire
To burn is already a burning!
How about that!

iii

Meanwhile the maple
Has also survived, and thinks
It owes its longevity

To its location
Between a bus stop
And a bar, and to its uniquely

Mutant appetite for pollutants:
Carbon monoxide, alcohol, spit . . .
The truth is, it enjoys city life.

Regular working people suffer so grossly
It makes a tree feel happier,
Having nothing to do

But feel its thousand orgasms each spring
Or stretch its limbs during the windy days
That are like a Swedish massage,

Or swoon into the fall
Among its delicious rain patters,
Its saffron and scarlet flamings.

Then, when the tethered leaves
Snatch themselves away like desperate
Adolescents ardent for freedom,

It will let itself sigh, feel wise
And resigned, and draw
Its thoughts downward to its other crown,

The secret leafless system
That digs in dark
Its thick intelligent arms

And stubborn hands
Under the shops, the streets,
The subways, the granite,

The sewage pipes'
Cold slime,
As deep as that.

❧ Helium

—for J.P.O.

For some reason you got up that morning
And decided your balloon was finally
Beginning to give up the ghost
Although, silver and blue, with its friendly caption,
"Happy Birthday," it had been hovering
Up at the ceiling for a month
Like a genial visitor from another planet.
Today you said, "Look, it's inches below the ceiling,"
And there were puckers in it like human skin,
Like the skin of old people.
I knew you were thinking of George, my mother's husband,
A third of a century older than us,
Forgetting to zip his fly, forgetting to wash
Or shave or wipe himself,
Saying and saying it to you: "Jerry, don't get old,"
Man to man, in a voice like someone banging
On a hollow pipe.
You were thinking about his bristly gray cheeks,
His desperate eyes, his advanced obsession with food,
So you cut the balloon's tether,
Pulled on a pair of pants
And we both went outside, still in bare feet,
To stand in the street and watch you release it.
It rose up slowly,
Missed the maples in our front yard, was caught
In a current of breeze and rose faster,
Was becoming distant from us,
Then darted behind a neighbor's copper beech
On the next block and we lost it.
After waiting awhile we took the *New York Times*
From the driveway and went on in for breakfast.
It was still springtime, the sun already high,
And your balloon was either still ascending
Or stopped in the arms of a tree. We couldn't know which,
And we were glad of this.

George in Hospital

For a while, in the hospital,
He could sit in his wheelchair, with his diapers tucked
Under green cotton gown,
And watch the people walking past his room.
It was lively and interesting. The nurses
Were pretty and brisk. The doctors were tall
And confident as princes. "Oh," he could say,
"These doctors are really tall. They're a tall bunch."
He could mislay my name, but ask
After my kids, faking it, saying
"Oh yeah, what sweethearts." He could ask:
"Can I please lie down in my bed now?"
He could raise his leathery yellowed feet:
"Can't somebody cut my toenails, please?
Oh, it's terrible." He could still
Push out a voice like traprock down a chute,
The hunks of gravel grating against metal,
To yell, "Oh Mary and Jesus,
This is terrible."

Excerpts from "A Birthday Suite"

—for Eve

The Cambridge Afternoon Was Gray

When you were born, the nurse's aide
Wore a gray uniform, and the Evelyn Nursing Home
Was full of Sisters of Mercy starched

To a religious ecstasy
Of tidiness. They brought you, struggling feebly
Inside your cotton blanket, only your eyes

Were looking as if you already knew
What thinking would be like—
Some pinch of thought was making your eyes brim

With diabolic relish, like a child
Who has been hiding crouched down in a closet
Among the woolen overcoats and stacked

Shoeboxes, while the anxious parents
Call *Where are you?* And suddenly the child
Bounces into the room

Pretending innocence. . . . My hot breast
Was delighted, and ran up to you like a dog
To a younger dog it wants to make friends with,

So the scandalized aide had to pull the gray
Curtains around our bed, making a sound
Of hissing virtue, curtainrings on rod,

While your eyes were saying *Where am I? I'm here!*

Bitterness

Somebody said of you when you were young,
"That child hates being a child"
—It explained or seemed to explain your resistance

To love, the creamy family food
I tried to dish out. So against my will
I had to look at you, the little daughter,

Where you sat glumly on bare linoleum
Hitting a block with another block,
Until I felt it, the humiliation

Of childhood helplessness, the dumbness
Of the giant omnivores who
Never listened, never understood,

Who always kept on shoving you around
For your own good. You looked
Settled as if you knew you were

The final piece of fruit
Left in a festive bowl while the noisy guests
Go right ahead with their toasting and spilling,

A solitary apple, unripe, stunted,
But keeping busy catalyzing the bitterness
Under its peel: an apple nobody wanted

Or was ever going to want.

Cat

If a cat can be ugly, Tiger was ugly.
A nothing color, the color of ash.
A coward, flinching

From anyone's shoes,
The desperate thin mind of a terrorist
As if we had plucked him from Belfast, biting

And clawing the hand that fed
Or attempted caress, drawing blood, inscribing
I will avenge in the long scratch marks

The wicked pee, the pitiable
Attacks of vomiting,
And you

Loved him, you alone loved him
The way we have to love the world, have to
Keep on loving it, like passing some kind of test

That God seems to be setting us. His bowls
Of Kitty Chow and water laid
By a clean litterbox, his fur petted,

You would pucker your brow, *good Tiger, good Tiger,*
Lifting him from the German prison camps
From the South American torturers to your lap

Smelling of young girl, making him see reason.

Design

Curled on the sofa she does her problem sets.
Her auburn hair cascades, her fingers write,
Her sighs heave, according to a formula

For which we'll never learn the equations.
Okay, what makes this phototropic tendril
Lift itself into air, place itself outward

So, upward so? Some code is being
Decoded in some control room, essential decisions
Are occurring every moment. The parents pretend

To go about their business, while casting
Furtive glances at the plant in their midst.
They have appeared to drive to work, come home,

Eat dinner and dessert. Actually,
They are holding onto the arboretum railing,
While the stalks emerge, fork,

Burst into leaves! Now they have almost forgotten
The way for years it was darkish prickles,
Tightest of wrappings, until

The thorn-leaves fell, and she stepped out like a girl
In a fairy tale, all stingless, all petals,
All infinite bits of pollen—

The elegant proof, the argument from design.

✌ Stream

With swift delusional energy:
That's how my best student in '67
Described a rushing

Stream, and I have forgotten
Neither the phrase nor his series
Of quick disintegrations over the next

Few years, a river dropping
Down a flight of steps. It wasn't the acid
He dropped in Vietnam did this, it was the people

He dropped,
That is to say he killed,
He and his army buddies, and took

Personally, I knew because his hands shook
If he tried to talk
About it, and then he'd stop

Out of deference to me perhaps:
Young, I had never seen a person's hands
Shaking. Maybe he'd tell

A bitter joke on the nuns
Who raised him in South Jersey,
Mocking their gestures, and then clutch

His body, small and strong
Like my husband's. I recall his tidy mustache,
The braying giggle that confused the other students

Before he dropped out. I recall there is
a difference between illusion
And delusion, the *maya*

That sustains us, flimsy ghosts in a flimsy world,
And the madness
And suffering that destroy us. The stream isn't

Delusional, I say, it represents
A truth, the actual motion of all matter,
All energy in its interior

Secret torrent that's invisible
To my stupid human
Eye, and it is also

The image of those minds
That smash one way, downhill,
Downhill, amid the spray

Of their uncontrollable
Meditations, downhill,
Slowly or swiftly

Without peace, without hope,
Letting themselves be broken, time
After time, by stone

After stone, and I believe the raging,
The flying water is real,
The tons of it, only

I hate the frozen snowfields
It descends from, a delusional
Purity, and the brutal

Rock that rends it,
A delusional
Solidity.

✒ The Pure Products of America

In the middle of the Southeast Asian war
When my poetry students would drive
Down from New Brunswick
To meet in my apartment,
See my family, sit on floor, drink wine—
This one sometimes might
Appear, dressed in his
Bob Dylan outfit, black
Scruffy boots, bluejeans, torn
Flannel shirt, black
Leather motorcycle jacket
And a black hat with a brim
To hide his timid face under.
He didn't talk. Late
In the evening he might extract
From his jeans pocket a many-folded
Piece of paper, and
Read the poem on it, a carnival
Or a barnyard, blowing us
Away. He wasn't actually
In the class, but nobody cared about
Things like that then, and Luke was good in ways
We liked, he despised the war, demanded sex
And love for all, in America's own
Vulgarly exhilarating speech
That cats and dogs can figure out,
Tamping it down with dynamite imagery,
Like Rimbaud, and with cadences
Out of rhythm and blues. We all knew
Boys like that. What happened
To this one, he went west
And somehow wrong, America the Beautiful
Too ugly or too toxic. Underwent
Some jail, some hospital, the medication,
The things the experts did then, when a person

Without a lot of money slid
Into the funny Asian jungle
That's right at home, to ensure
They would never return
With information for us. Luke still writes
Me letters, it's about twenty years,
Pages half legible in a childish hand.
He thinks he's a detective, only
They put poison in my head
Is what he says, *It*
Slows me down, baby, the therapy—
I used to write him back
But I wish he'd quit.

✿ Windshield

You are supposed to roll your windows up
Driving through certain neighborhoods
Because they are waiting for you at the intersections,
For you or anyone,
Where cars go bumper to bumper,
Flirtatious shadows, wanting to clean your windshield,
Perhaps, or to shoot you, the way they shot my friend
The talkative flutist, lost on Detroit's avenues,
Through his open old Ford window.
Got him in the cheek and shoulder,
No reason. He was just busy talking, and the summer
Evening was stifling.
Up at the red light now, they are doing their crisp dance
With their rags and squeegees
Around a helpless Subaru.
Watch it, mister—
A warrior strut, a cottonmouth snap to remind you
Of the wet odor of rural underbrush,
A little twirl, a little
Hustle on oily cobblestones.
When one of them advances on you, yellow eyes
And shining teeth, denim slung
Low on a wasted pelvis, you can feel
In your bones the awful
Cruelty of his life,
Nothing to lose—
As looking at you sitting behind windowglass
Just at the moment you resist the urge
Your foot has, to jam on the gas,
He sees that blank expression flattening
Your face like a heavy drug, and he
Can feel the cruelty
Of yours, man, right in his bones.

❧ The Bride

i

Jerusalem sits on her mountains, a woman
Who knits and frowns, going over and over her story,
Sifting it, every detail memorized, magnified,
Interpreted. How many lovers, what caresses, what golden
Fornications, what children of brilliant intellect
Sucking hard at her nipples,
What warriors, what artists.

There was a time for riches, a time for poverty.
She has gone begging in the streets, yes,
And she has danced in her rags.

And today they are killing for her
Among the stones. What woman would not
Be thoroughly proud. They love her, they love her
Above the queens
Of the earth, above the other beauties.

ii

The cats in Jerusalem form the secret
Government. They are sisters. They have hearts
As black as eels, or hearts as red
And wise as pomegranates.
They insinuate everywhere, everywhere.
Under the shady orange trees
Sit three or four,
By the ruined wall a score,
Nine surround the Dome of the Rock.
Six yawn, their mouths open as orchids,
Revealing needle teeth.

So forget the rabbis and their frozen Law,
A rod that likes

Hitting a child's fingers, and making
That satisfying sting of punishment.
Forget about the members
Of Parliament, shouting yet reasonable
Like jewelry merchants counting on your goodwill.
Forget the competitive brands of Christians
Selling postcards of sexy crucifixions
Who peer from shadowy galleries of the Church
Of the Holy Sepulchre, its livid saints
And martyrs dissolving into grimy mosaic darkness.
Forget the revolutionary students.
Cheap thrills, cheap thrills.
Forget even the fleshy mothers
Sarah and Hagar,
Praying, shopping, cooking,
Complaining. Forget their apartments, their leaky
Sinks, and the shortened screams when the bad news comes
On the evening radio about their sons
Who were tall and handsome, who were slightly careless
In Hebron, or the Golan, or Beirut.

Forget the mayor, his rosy stitching and patching.
Forget making the world a better place.

Blood and sand.
What is reality and what is fiction?
The cats crouch, the cats
Have a saying: You've seen one corpse,
You've seen them all. The black, the white, the gray,
Stealthy, overt, and sleek,
The runners, the striped ones,
The ones that look like apricots and milk,
Are receiving orders from a small, blackened
Bronze Egyptian cat
In the Rockefeller Museum
Near the Damascus gate,

The cat of dire memory, whose heart,
The size of an olive, is heavier
Than an iron cannonball.

Heavy because so angry,
So angry.

❧ The Death Ghazals

If a raindrop enters the ocean, good.
It is where it yearned to be.

If it enters the soil, good.
Let's hope something will grow.

They thought like this for thousands of years
While the clean dead refreshed the ground.

Heroes lay with the ash-spears through their brains
And Homer sang of them, striking the harp.

Stomachs of girls forgot the hours of childbirth
Under the lawns, in the swept tombs.

The skin of the deeply old, among stones,
Kept helping the lovers to kiss.

Today even the rainstorms are poisoned—
Bleak dust, a sterilized lake, infected forests—

Ghostly buffalo stand in your car's headlights
And you drive right through them.

ii

Something exciting is kicking through the sperm,
The capillaries, the plasma, and now it's home.

They love this house! They've dusted and polished, they've brought
Their own expensive silver.

The committeemen loosen their neckties, there ought to be
A law, or so they claim. They arrange their papers.

Hath the rain a father? Shall we seal the border?
Nature is a law also, like *need,* like *night.*

Like a needle, the word *death*
Is easily mislaid. The word *pestilential.*

Ripe bloodspots, there and there, on the moon's face,
Make her a swollen whore, and no more maiden.

Three-deep along the leather bar, a jacket, a hip, a saxophone
Wails and rotates on its gummy axle.

For sticks and rags, try looking at a puppet
When the master removes his hand.

iii

—D. K., 1932–1986

Now your old teacher and friend
Is traveling the highway backward.

Straight as a yardstick, it runs toward a canal
Where a boat bumps gently against logs.

Billboards wing past, offering salutations,
Two crows alight on a telephone wire.

Palaces, churches, a glorious morning
Ripens toward noon, even in narrow alleyways.

He is trying to hold his head high
As the water smell approaches.

He is pink
And hairless, like a newborn mouse.

Are you ready to pray yet? Are you ready to light candles?
Closer. Come on closer. Are you ready to go to the concert?

iv

—for Suzanne Vega

Whatever doesn't suffer isn't alive.
Student number one, will you kindly comment?

Increased consciousness: potential for charm and sanity,
For acute pain, for self and others. Your choice.

A holier healing, a more efficient torture—
Remind me if this is the dance of Shiva.

I'm trying to remember something. Wasn't it illumination,
The crests of sex?

Girl of ice at the party, you stand at the bathroom sink,
Throwing up your bitterness, along with your last drink.

Papa, you gave her a silk dress from Saigon,
Saying, "Don't ask me where I got it from."

"The exalted mirror can go to hell," laugh the courtesans
Of Greece, and Italy, and imperial China.

Where there's life there's hope. We bequeath this hope
To our children, along with our warm tears.

v

And I won't even mention the crying of orphans
that reaches up to the throne of God and
beyond, making
a circle with no end and no god.
— *Yehudah Amichai*

Not having found you in music or mathematics
They look for you, my God, on the battlefield.

Blind fiery hope propels them,
A Promethean gift, an illusion.

"You can't see anything through the fire
But the fire itself, and it's so smoky."

"And the intense heat when you approach
Hurls you backward, but it's so marvelous."

Bodies of brothers dropping like soot.
High in the air, gunfire rattle and cannon hoot.

Ecstasy of pain, drawn across the dirt
Into which it is coughing blood, to the Red Cross station—

Clad in ironic olive, on both sides
Boys fight, who have scarcely learned to shave—

At last they feel alive! They have discovered
What they were made for, from the very cradle.

Amid carnage they are altogether joyous
For they believe they see you striding there.

Is it true, is it true, are you a champion?
Does your smeared forehead out-top the gracious mountain?

A Meditation in Seven Days

i

Hear O Israel
the Lord our God
the Lord is One
—*Deuteronomy* 6:4

If your mother is a Jew, you are a Jew
—Here is the unpredictable

Residue, but of what archaic power
Why the chain of this nation matrilineal

When the Holy One, the One
Who creates heaven and earth from formless void

Is utterly, violently masculine, with his chosen
Fathers and judges, his kings

And priests in their ritual linen, their gold and blue,
And purple and scarlet, his prophets clothed only

In a ragged vision of righteousness, angry
Voices promising a destructive fire

And even in exile, his rabbis with their flaming eyes
The small boys sent to the house of study

To sit on the benches
To recite, with their soft lips, a sacred language

To become the vessels of memory,
Of learning, of prayer,

Across the vast lands of the earth, kissing
His Book, though martyred, though twisted

Into starving rags, in
The village mud, or in wealth and grandeur

Kissing his Book, and the words of the Lord
Became fire on their lips

—What were they all but men in the image
Of God, where is their mother

∾

The lines of another story, inscribed
And reinscribed like an endless chain

A proud old woman, her face desert-bitten
Has named her son: laughter

Laughter for bodily pleasure, laughter for old age triumph
Hagar the rival stumbles away

In the hot sand, along with her son Ishmael
They nearly die of thirst, God pities them

But among us each son and daughter
Is the child of Sarah, whom God made to laugh

∾

Sarah, legitimate wife
Woman of power

My mother is a Jew, I am a Jew
Does it teach me enough

In the taste of every truth a sweeter truth
In the bowels of every injustice an older injustice

In memory
A tangle of sandy footprints

ii

Whoever teaches his daughter Torah, teaches her obscenity.
—*Rabbi Eleazer*

If a woman is a Jew
Of what is she the vessel

If she is unclean in her sex, if she is
Created to be a defilement and a temptation

A snake with breasts like a female
A succubus, a flying vagina

So that the singing of God
The secret of God

The name winged in the hues of the rainbow
Is withheld from her, so that she is the unschooled

Property of her father, then of her husband
And if no man beside her husband

May lawfully touch her hand
Or gaze at her almond eyes, if when the dancers

Ecstatically dance, it is not with her,
Of what is she the vessel

If a curtain divides her prayer
From a man's prayer

We shall burn incense to the queen of heaven, and shall pour her
libations as we used to do, we, our fathers, our kings and our
princes, in the cities of Judah and the streets of Jerusalem. For
then we had plenty of food and we were all well and saw no evil.
                            —*Jeremiah* 44:17

Solomon's foreign wives, and the Canaanite daughters
Who with Ishtar mourned the death of Tammuz

Who *on the high places, under every green tree, and alongside*
The altars set fig boughs, images of Ashtoreth

Who *offered incense to the queen of heaven*
And sang in a corner of the temple, passing from hand to hand

In token of joy the fruited branch, body
Of the goddess their mothers loved

Who made cakes bearing her features
And their husbands knew

The Lady of Snakes
The Lady of Lilies

She who makes prosper the house
Who promulgates goodness, without whom is famine

Cursed by the furious prophet, scattered screaming
Burned alive according to law, for witchcraft

Stoned to death by her brothers, perhaps by men
She has nakedly loved, for the free act of love

In her city square
Her eyes finally downcast

Her head shaved
Is she too the vessel of memory

iv

For out of Zion shall go forth the law, and the word of the Lord
from Jerusalem. And he shall judge among the nations, and shall
rebuke many people: and they shall beat their swords into plow-
shares, and their spears into pruning hooks: nation shall not lift
up sword against nation, neither shall they learn war any more.

    —Isaiah 2:3–4

Here is another story: the ark burned,
The marble pillars buried, the remnant scattered

A thousand years, two thousand years
In every patch of the globe, the gentle remnant

Of whom our rabbis boast: *Compassionate sons
Of compassionate fathers*

In love not with the Law, but with the kindness
They claim to be the whole of the Torah

Torn from a whole cloth
From the hills of Judea

That ran with sweetness, and from the streams
That were jewels, yearning for wholeness, next

Year in Jerusalem, surely, there would be
Milk and honey, they could see

The thing plainly, an ideal society
Of workers, the wise, the holy hill flowing

Finally with righteousness—
Here they are, in the photographs of the 1880s,

The young women, with their serious eyes
Their lace collars and cameo brooches

Are the partners of these serious young men
Who stand shaven, who have combed their hair smoothly

They are writing pamphlets together, which describe
In many little stitches the word *shalom*

They have climbed out of the gloomy villages
They have kissed the rigid parents good-bye

Soon they will be a light to the nations
They will make the desert bloom, they are going to form

The plough and pruninghook Isaiah promised
After tears of fire, of blood, of mud

Of the sword and shame
Eighty generations

Here in their eyes the light of justice from Sinai
And the light of pure reason from Europe

v

Does the unanswered prayer
Corrode the tissue of heaven

Doesn't it rust the wings
Of the heavenly host, shouldn't it

Untune their music, doesn't it become
Acid splashed in the face of the king

Smoke, and the charred bone bits suspended in it
Sifting inevitably upward

Spoiling paradise
Spoiling even the dream of paradise

vi

Come, my friend, come, my friend
Let us go to meet the bride.
—*Sabbath Song*

And in between she would work and clean and cook. But
the food, the food. . . . O the visits were filled with food.
—*Melanie Kaye/Kantrowitz*

Not speculation, nothing remote
No words addressed to an atomic father

Not the wisdom of the wise
Nor a promise, and not the trap of hereafter

Here, now, through the misted kitchen windows
Since dawn the dusk is falling

Everywhere in the neighborhood
Women have rushed to the butcher, the grocer

With a violet sky she prepares the bread, she plucks
And cooks the chicken, grates the stinging horseradish

These are her fingers, her sinewy back as she scrubs
The house, her hands slap the children and clean them

Dusk approaches, wind moans
Food ready, it is around her hands

The family faces gather, the homeless
She has gathered like sheep, it is her veiny hands

That light the candles, so that suddenly
Our human grief illuminated, we're a circle

Practical and magical, it's
Strong wine and food time coming, and from outside time

From the jeweled throne
Of a house behind history

She beckons the bride, the radiant
Sabbath, the lady we share with God

Our mother's palms like branches lifted in prayer
Lead our rejoicing voices, our small chorus

Our clapping hands in the here and now
In a world that is never over

And never enough

vii

> For lo, the winter is past; the rain is over and gone;
> The flowers appear on the earth; the time of the
> singing of birds is come.
>
> —*Song of Solomon 2:11–12*

What can I possess
But the history that possesses me

With whom must I wrestle
But myself

And as to the father, what is his trouble
That leaves him so exhausted and powerless

Why is he asleep, his gigantic
Limbs pulseless, dispersed over the sky

White, unnerved
No more roar

He who yesterday threatened murder, yanking
On his old uniform, waving his dress sword

He's broken every glass in the house, the drunkard
He's snapped the sticks of furniture, howling

And crying, liquor spilled everywhere
He's staggered to the floor, and lies there

In filth, three timid children prod him
While screwing their faces up from the stink

That emanates from his mouth—
He has beaten them black and blue

But they still love him, for
What other father have they, what other king—

He begins to snore, he is dreaming again
How outside the door a barefoot woman is knocking

Snakes slide downhill in the forest
Preparing to peel themselves in rebirth, wriggling

Fiddlehead ferns uncurl, a square of blue sky
Flings its veil, pale mushrooms

Raise their noses after the downpour
A breeze rustles through her yellow dress

Don't come back, he whispers in his sleep
Like a man who endures a nightmare

And in my sleep, in my twentieth century bed
It's that whisper I hear, *go away,*

Don't touch, so that I ask
of what am I the vessel

Fearful, I see my hand is on the latch
I am the woman, and about to enter

Excerpts from "Homage to Rumi"

The Armies of Birds

While we were asleep, the armies
Of birds arrived, and are filling the world with song.
That flat, miserable brownness
We remember has vanished.
The first blue crocuses struggle
From under the earth and kneel
In the sunlight. Get up,
Get dressed, friend!
The police are throwing their caps
And badges away.

Whoever stays sober in this weather
Is afraid of what the neighbors will say.

I Can't Speak

God is the Being . . . that may properly only be addressed,
not expressed.

—*Martin Buber,* I and Thou

It's hopeless. Our heads are full of television
But images fall apart when you enter a room.
And if not television, then words.
Poets, philosophers, intellectuals, theologians—
Can any of us truly love you?
I want to talk about kissing the small piece
Of nameless, edgeless geometry you've shown me
And how grateful I am. But should I say I'm the pond
A star fell into, or a rock?

Anyway, I can't speak about you,
Only to you, there's the whole trouble,
As if, when I tried to turn my body aside,
Some absolute force twisted it back around.
If I insist, *It's my body, my mind,*
My own mouth, I'll say what I want,
I have the right to,
You simply smile.

What You've Given Me

What's worse than having no word from you?
— *Rumi*

For my birthday, you came over laughing,
Set down a box with a present in it
And went away laughing.

I know what you've given me
Is inside. But sometimes I'm frightened
I'll spend my entire life

Like this, pulling off tissue
Wrappings, and never
Come to the present.

What You Want

A half a dozen times in my existence
You have permitted me to glimpse
Some portion of you—

The morning I lay in the bathtub
Very pregnant, and my body was
Mount Moriah, before the people
Or the goat, or the god.
The afternoon my infant son
Kicking his chubby legs
While I diapered him was also the divine
Baby, hurtling
Coldly toward me from the other world
Where everything is lightning.

The night my father
Let me know he wasn't gone
Just because he was dead, a couple of times
When a man set down his sword to let me in
To the orchard and vineyard, and the night
I was driving happy, and saw a woman
In a white gown, dancing
Where my windshield was.

No words, only supreme
Joy at being visited.

Friend, I could say
I've been alive a half dozen moments
　　　　but that's not true
　　　　I've been alive my entire time
　　　　　　on this earth
　　　　I've been alive

—That's what you want me to say, isn't it.

What's Your Name

When I call you the One
You glance over your shoulder,
Half sneering
Like a big celebrity,
And I know you're bored.

When I call you the Many
you are suddenly here kissing me
From my feet to my mouth,
Or you're telling me funny stories
Drying my tears.

They say I should try calling you Nothing—
But I don't know
If I'm ready for that yet.

✍ To Love Is

You do not need to accomplish the work; nor
are you free to desist from it.
—*The Ethics of the Fathers*

i

To love is
To desire the liberty
Of the one loved

The lover thinking *Take me*
With you wherever you go
Of your own free will

Wanting to join
The dancing, the drunkenness, the kissing
On the roof, under the moon

But not to force it, not
To beg for it,
Not to be afraid it is a lie.

ii

Why all this crying?
The separated lovers
Believe they need each other

And the rejected one
Would like to hurl the rafters
Of buildings down

Or tear the mask away from a certain face
Because of its look of contempt,
While all the time

There is only the one need.

iii

And if I have desired
Since my first childish moments of sentience
When I recognized that I ardently loved the world

The balanced radiance of its good and evil
And wanted to help unlock it to become
More and more itself—

More and more alive—
What then? As I grow older
I love it less, the evil seems denser,

More strangely skewed,
My world nastier and myself weaker.
Still I keep my original loyalty,

My memory—a child on a busy
Sidewalk looking around and thinking
Beautiful dirty city, beautiful planet

I have my task,
What matter if I can
Never accomplish it.

✃ Move

Whether it's a turtle who drags herself
Slowly to the sandlot where she digs
The sandy nest she was born to dig

And lay leathery eggs in, or whether it's salmon
Rocketing upstream
Toward pools that call: *Bring your eggs here*

And nowhere else in the world, whether it is turtle-green
Ugliness and awkwardness, or the seething
Grace and gild of silky salmon, we

Are envious, our wishes speak out right here
Thirsty for a destiny like theirs,
An absolute right choice

To end all choices. Is it memory,
We ask, is it a smell
They remember

Or just what is it, some kind of blueprint
That makes them move, hot grain by grain,
Cold cascade above icy cascade,

Slipping through
Water's fingers
A hundred miles

Inland from the easy shiny sea—
And we also, in the company
Of our tribe

Or perhaps alone, like the turtle
On her wrinkled feet with the tapping nails,
We also are going to travel, we say let's be

Oblivious to all, save
That we travel, and we say
When we reach the place we'll know

We are in the right spot, somehow, like a breath
Entering a singer's chest, that shapes itself
For the song that is to follow.

 The Crack in Everything
(1996)

The Dogs at Live Oak Beach, Santa Cruz

As if there could be a world
Of absolute innocence
In which we forget ourselves

The owners throw sticks
And half-bald tennis balls
Toward the surf
And the happy dogs leap after them
As if catapulted—

Black dogs, tan dogs,
Tubes of glorious muscle—

Pursuing pleasure
More than obedience
They race, skid to a halt in the wet sand,
Sometimes they'll plunge straight into
The foaming breakers

Like diving birds, letting the green turbulence
Toss them, until they snap and sink

Teeth into floating wood
Then bound back to their owners
Shining wet, with passionate speed
For nothing,
For absolutely nothing but joy.

❧ Boil

Boil over—it's what the nerves do,
Watch them seethe when stimulated,

Murmurs the man at the stove
To the one at the fridge—

Watch that electric impulse that finally makes them
Fume and fizz at either

Frayed end. If you could grasp a bundle
Of nerves in your fist like a jumper cable, and sense that

Python's writhe, or a garden hose when the pressure's
High and it wilfully weaves about

Trying its best to get away from you—
You'd see how nothing is passive,

We're all—I mean from our elephant sun, ejaculant
Great-grandfather, cascading down

To weightless
Unstoppable neutrinos

Leaving their silvery trace
In vacuum chambers, in

Effervescent lines, twisted
Madly in our madhouse jackets,

Rules, laws, which we are seething to break
Though to rupture them might be of course to die,

Or, *possibly,*
To change:

Boil, it's what water
And everything else teaches.

Marie at Tea

You remember the extremes
Wittgenstein says
There is no such thing as ordinary
Experience

My heart aches, literally, and a drowsy
So I wonder if I will die soon
Sometimes I am so tired
I want to

You remember the extremes
I remember when his father died
We took the train into London
Sat in his childhood
And boyhood parlor
Listened to a Joan Baez record
That we always listened to
And when she began singing
"The Great Silkie," a tragic
Scottish folk song about fathers
And sons, he threw
his head in my lap and sobbed, I
Never saw him weep again although
I have sobbed and yowled countless times
On his chest his lap his shoulder
I remember when I gave birth
The first time, thirty-six hours in labor
While he was sitting in the labor room
Trying to help me breathe
Through my contractions
Then in a corner reading an
Obstetrics textbook where
Normal childbirth occupied
Fifty pages and possible complications
Five hundred pages
It frightened him so terribly he wanted

To tell the obstetrician if he had a choice
To let the baby go and save his wife
I have always felt
This to be touching
I remember the lunch in the Red Lion
When in tears I begged him
To stop fooling around with the au pair girl
And to my astonishment
He refused. You remember
The extreme things
Not the normal
Uneventful moments
Years decades
Food sex
Screams laughter
Betrayal conciliation
A day at the races
A night at the opera
Everything slightly cracked
Then afterwards you say:
We're married this long
Because we are both too stubborn
To admit we made a mistake,
Which is a good line
And a workable disguise

The truth is that you do not know the truth

The kernel of death
Life wraps itself around
Like chamois cloth
Around a diamond

Ice
Cold at the center
Precious no doubt because

Inhumanly old, that
Is my idea of
Love, of marriage, the
Extreme

🙠 Migrant

Desire comes up in us
Like the morning sun
Over the Great Central Valley

Perfectly dry and stark
Diagonal rays gilding the fields
And the insects waking in them

The sun sheds a pink light
On the adobe streets—
On the dust—

Not yet aroused
We breathe with ravishment
The cool, blue, untainted inland air

We are already sweating
As we tramp from our trailers
Toward ripeness a mile off

Facing the anger of the sun
The light sound of a motor approaching
And receding is still pleasant

So few people as yet
Getting into their cars and going to work
Blackbirds are audible, we feel like men

Until the moment we bend
Over the stalks, and there it is—
Pain cruises up

With its hot knives,
Its rotten burlap sacks,
Like changing a channel

To a show that has always been playing.

✑ Globule

It is like what we imagine knowledge to be.
—*Elizabeth Bishop*

i

To be transparent, to contain the world,
To be jellyfish, lucent, mobile, membraned,

Boneless behold me, my mica bits
Expensive steel suspended in my substance,

Afloat in floodwater, swinging shoreward,
Ebbing oceanward, clockless among quick fishes—

Striped, spotted,
Speckled, stippled—

Swishing between braincoral cobbles,
Granulated brine, ever in motion.

ii

From plate tinted a shell's hard innerness,
Cerise bleeds, leads chilly dawn.

Sunlight struggles downward through wavelets
Near the sound's warm surface, visible even

From the cliffs of cottages, it pushes relentlessly
Finding us, feeding us, diatoms, sea-lace,

Anemones, kelp. Breathing in our beds,
Bright sunlight sustains us, formidable father,

We who are oblivious, maybe immortal,
Then softens, slants, abruptly dips. There's darkness.

Brutally cold, the boom of surf unheard,
Over pocked sand, purely indifferent,

Rock ridges ready to razor tenderness,
Seawater keeps moving forgetfully.

iii

Now on the surface moonlight rests like ice,
And the far sky blinks its pointed messages,

Pointless to me, about matter's beginnings—
Membraneous, shapeless, rocking undersea,

Both a thing contained and container of mystery,
Smoothness inside of smoothness, cold in cold,

Wishing only to be as I am, transparent,
Textured fleck afloat in a wet world.

❧ Nude Descending

Like a bowerbird trailing a beakful of weeds
Like prize ribbons for the very best

The lover, producer
Of another's pleasure

He whom her swollen lips await
Might wing through any day of the decade

A form of health insurance
For which it is never too late

Titanic, silver brush
Hindenburg, of exploding cigars a climax

The watery below, the fiery above
Ashes of print between—pigment between

If the crippled woman were to descend
From her bed, her fortress beyond midnight

Downstairs *(nude/staircase)* to the kitchen
Naked to sit at the table *(writing/thinking)*

She might hear the washer spin like a full orchestra
Complete a cycle like a train crash

Before the fiend would stare through the window
Step smoothly into the kitchen, stop some clocks.

Envy shapes a fig tree in one's breast,
That is, bluntly to say, a cancer,

That is to say
In a mind, a fertile windy field. A murdered child.

Well then, fear, primarily of falling.
Ebony surf toils on the beach, a glaze

At the same moment I am *(from a cliff)* falling
The kitchen fiend removes his Dior tie

Places his hand over the woman's
And softly says: I am the lover.

Now if the crippled woman began to dance
To pirouette, to rumba

Growling for her child
Her burning page, the devil would be shamed

*(Materialism is not for everyone / Religion is
The extension of politics by other means)*

Would disembody like a wicked smoke
Back to the status of myth

Away he'd streak, blue, into the—
O faun, we would finally call, farewell

O faun, we would faintly faintly call
O faun, we would, we would fondly—

She does not dance. She does not wish
To produce another's pleasure.

They have torn her apart
Into beige rectangles.

The Studio (Homage to Alice Neel)

An oily rag at her feet in the warehouse of scents
Releases essence of pine. A steampipe knocks.
A radio urges the purchase of Philip Morris Cigarettes,
Ford motor cars, Saks quality slipcovers.
Welcome to America, Grand Central Station,
Crossroads of a nation. There is no heaven and no hell,

You got to understand, this existence is it,
I blame nobody, I just paint, paint is thicker than water,
Blood, or dollars. My friends and neighbors are made
Of paint, would you believe it, paintslabs and brushstrokes
Right down to the kishkes, as my grandfather would say.
Like bandaged Andy, not smart enough to duck.

Palette knife jabs, carnation, ocher, viridian.
Look at them. And look at me, I'm like Rembrandt,
Poor, omnivorous, and made of pity. Made of love.
Like José on the couch with nostrils like Dante's inferno.
The thing about life in the bughouse, says Alice Neel,
Is it's better than killing yourself. And you get some rest.

Insane asylum, bughouse, madhouse, loony bin,
Snake pit, it's like the Eskimo words for snow.
I never appreciated the nuances though.
After a while the life is only boring.
The food condenses to pudding.
The beds were cold oatmeal in the first place.

The unconscious cruelties of the staff cease to amuse you.
And when you find yourself secretly peeking
Through the window bars at menstrual red sunsets,
You decide you cannot tolerate the other loonies another day.
So you behave sanely and leave. Bye-bye!
And you're back in the basement studio.

✥ Appearance and Reality

—in memory of May Swenson

Amphibian, crustacean? The nooked neck
Seems always in process of peering

Hesitantly out, or rapidly withdrawing,
Pulling its loose pleats tight again

Back in its turtle shell. It's like a hand
Puppet returned to its lacquered box,

Or a ferocious child imprisoned in
Shyness, but what if we picture

That same child, some long-ago July
In her Utah backyard examining a turtle

That feigns nonentity itself? Tapping it
Where it lies in the pool of her pinafore

With a fingernail to hear the tick,
She has to chuckle. She admires the dish shape,

Checks its polished markings, turns it over
To look at the tough olive underside,

Peers for the claws, the scratchy nails, and then
She wants to see its pursy face.

Shyness pink as the inside of a mouth,
A mouth maybe with many sharpened teeth

And black sandpaper tongue, rough like a cat's,
Worth waiting for. But when the beast emerges,

Not interested in her, it begins instantly
To row away, off her pink cotton

Lap and across the dandelioned lawn,
Headed beyond the painted fence and sunlit

Sidewalk, and makes its escape underneath
The shadow of the blue Nash at the curb.

Quite gone, it leaves her the memory
Of weight and scurry, of dangled unmapped day.

So the child gets set to travel everywhere,
To take a trip by staying still, to take

The planet in, in fond curiosity—
Can it be true she never went anywhere?

For here she is, her tan face elderly
And infantile at once, mixed like geology,

A pleated map or complicated sphere
Under a cap of ash blond baby-hair

Blunt-cut, and so fine that the least breeze
Can lift up tender wisps of it,

Like bits of chick-fluff or kitten fur,
She's feigning innocence, and letting wander

A pair of blue and stainless eyes,
Almost unlashed, bright as a baby bird's,

On a stocky body (like a Chinese lady's
In a kitchen) private and unembarrassed,

That curious face keeps cheering itself
By watching stuff. It's friendly. Really a mammal.

The Boys, the Broom Handle, the Retarded Girl

Who was asking for it—
Everyone can see
Even today in the formal courtroom,
Beneath the coarse flag draped
Across the wall like something on a stage,
Which reminds her of the agony of school
But also of a dress that they let her wear
To a parade one time,
Anyone can tell
She's asking, she's pleading
For it, as we all
Plead—
Chews on a wisp of hair,
Holds down the knee
That tries to creep under her chin,
Picks at a flake of skin, anxious
And eager to please this scowling man
And the rest of them, if she only can—
Replies *I cared for them, they were my friends*

It is she of whom these boys
Said, afterward, *Wow, what a sicko*
It is she of whom they boasted
As we all boast
Now and again, because we need,
Don't we, to feel
Worthwhile—
As without thinking we might touch for luck
That flag they've hung there, though we'd all avoid
Touching the girl.

The Eighth and Thirteenth

The Eighth of Shostakovich,
Music about the worst
Horror history offers,
They played on public radio
Again last night. In solitude
I sipped my wine, I drank
That somber symphony
To the vile lees. The composer
Draws out the minor thirds, the brass
Tumbles overhead like virgin logs
Felled from their forest, washing downriver,
And the rivermen at song. Like ravens
Who know when meat is in the offing,
Oboes form a ring. An avalanche
Of iron violins. At Leningrad
During the years of siege
Between bombardment, hunger,
And three subfreezing winters,
Three million dead were born
Out of Christ's bloody side. Like icy
Fetuses. For months
One could not bury them, the earth
And they alike were adamant.
You stacked the dead like sticks until May's mud,
When, of course, there was pestilence.
But the music continues. It has no other choice.
Stalin hated the music and forbade it.
Not patriotic, not Russian, not Soviet.
But the music continues. It has no other choice.
Peer in as far as you like, it stays
Exactly as bleak as now. The composer
Opens his notebook. *Tyrants like to present themselves as*
patrons of the arts. That's a well known fact. But tyrants
understand nothing about art. Why? Because tyranny is a
perversion and a tyrant is a pervert. He is attracted by the

chance to crush people, to mock them, stepping over
corpses. . . . And so, having satisfied his perverted desires,
the man becomes a leader, and now the perversions continue
because power has to be defended against madmen like
yourself. For even if there are no such enemies, you have
to invent them, because otherwise you can't flex your
muscles completely, you can't oppress the people completely,
making the blood spurt. And without that, what pleasure is
there in power? Very little. The composer
Looks out the door of his dacha, it's April,
He watches farm children at play,
He forgets nothing. For the thirteenth—
I slip its cassette into my car
Radio—they made Kiev's Jews undress
After a march to the suburb,
Shot the hesitant quickly,
Battered some of the lame,
And screamed at everyone.
Valises were taken, would
Not be needed, packed
So abruptly, tied with such
Frayed rope. Soldiers next
Killed a few more. The living ones,
Penises of the men like string,
Breasts of the women bobbling
As at athletics, were told to run
Through a copse, to where
Wet with saliva
The ravine opened her mouth.
Marksmen shot the remainder
Then, there, by the tens of thousands,
Cleverly, so that bodies toppled
In without lugging. An officer
Strode upon the dead,
Shot what stirred.

How it would feel, such uneasy
Footing, even wearing boots
That caressed one's calves, leather
and lambswool, the soles thick rubber,
Such the music's patient inquiry.
What then is the essence of reality?
Of the good? The mind's fuse sputters,
The heart aborts, it smells like wet ashes,
The hands lift to cover their eyes,
Only the music continues. We'll try,
For the first movement,
A full chorus.
The immediate reverse of Beethoven.
An axe between the shoulder blades
Of Herr Wagner. *People knew about Babi Yar
before Yevtushenko's poem, but they were silent. And when
they read the poem, the silence was broken. Art destroys
silence. I know that many will not agree with me and will
point out other, more noble aims of art. They'll talk about beauty,
grace, and other high qualities. But you won't catch
me with that bait. I'm like Sobakevich in* Dead Souls: *you can
sugarcoat a toad, and I still won't put it in my mouth.*

Most of my symphonies are tombstones, said Shostakovich.

All poets are Jews, said Tsvetaeva.

The words *never again*
Clashing against the words
Again and again
—That music.

✑ Saturday Night

> Music is most sovereign because more than anything
> else, rhythm and harmony find their way to the inmost
> soul and take strongest hold upon it, bringing with
> them and imparting grace.
>
> —*Plato,* The Republic

> The cranes are flying . . .
>
> *Chekhov*

And here it comes: around the world,
In Chicago, Petersburg, Tokyo, the dancers
Hit the floor running (the communal dancefloor

Here, there, at intervals, sometimes paved,
Sometimes rotted linoleum awash in beer,
Sometimes a field across which the dancers streak

Like violets across grass, sometimes packed dirt
In a township of corrugated metal roofs)
And what was once prescribed ritual, the profuse

Strains of premeditated art, is now improvisation,
The desperately new, where to the sine-curved
Yelps and spasms of police sirens outside

The club, a spasmodic feedback ululates
The death and cremation of history,
Until a boy whose hair is purple spikes,

And a girl wearing a skull
That wants to say *I'm cool but I'm in pain,*
Get up and dance together, sort of, age thirteen.

Young allegorists, they'll mime motions
Of shootouts, of tortured ones in basements,
Of cold insinuations before sex

Between enemies, the jubilance of the criminal.
The girl tosses her head and dances
The shoplifter's meanness and self-betrayal

For a pair of stockings, a scarf, a perfume,
The boy dances stealing the truck,
Shooting his father.

The point is to become a flying viper,
A diving vulva, the great point
Is experiment, like pollen flinging itself

Into far other habitats, or seed
That travels a migrant bird's gut
To be shit overseas.

The creatures gamble on the whirl of life
And every adolescent body hot
Enough to sweat it out on the dance floor

Is a laboratory: maybe this lipstick, these boots,
These jeans, these earrings, maybe if I flip
My hair and vibrate my pelvis

Exactly synched to the band's wildfire noise
That imitates history's catastrophe
Nuke for nuke, maybe I'll survive,

Maybe we'll all survive. . . .

At the intersection of poverty and plague
The planet's children—brave, uncontrollable, juiced
Out of their gourds—invent the sacred dance.

The Book of Life

—for Sheila Solomon

i

Everything very hardy.
Irises one surprise after another—the florist
Gave me the bulbs cheap, he didn't know their colors,
Big lavender with ruffly Victorian edges,
Pansies, then pinks, gaillardias, yellow with maroon edges and
Maroon centers, all perennials.

Then marigolds orange and gold, and alyssum.
Then I transplanted the beach rose, one of a pair
I bought for Cynthia, so healthy it was breaking the pot—

A blazing fall. The Days of Awe. A Book
Lies open on God's knee, God's ear
Is funneling repentances, but we
Are not in synagogue. Instead we stroll
Through mud around the pool you have bulldozed
In the bright wilderness of your back yard.
Gripping a trowel, you promise me you will swim
Daily. You will draw. You will take long
Walks by the bay.

This is the year your mother finally
Went blind, stamping and screaming *I can see*
Perfectly well and *This is your fault*
While you wept and telephoned nurses and lawyers.
It is the year your favorite uncle died,
He who taught you your first Jewish jokes
And called America *hopeless, politicians*
In bed with profiteers—where he came from, if you saw a Jew
Eating a chicken, you knew one of them was sick.
The year your daughter left for Oregon
To escape you, while you cramp over with dread
Of crowded arteries that could
Any time worsen—

Now we are arm in arm, I stroke your hand
Recalling an old photo of our daughters,
Three slippery toddlers in a bathtub.
Nina looks at the camera with the curious
Eyes of a faun, Rebecca smirks, Eve paddles
In the vicinity of her cozy belly
—If we could reach into that picture,
Splash them teasingly, touch their skin—

You say: *I go into my studio*
And can't recognize it.
What is this place, what did I mean to do,
Will I ever work again.

ii

We know the myth of the artist dying young
Consumptive, crazy,
The lyric poet melting back
Like a jack-in-the-pulpit in April woods,
Created by one rain shower,
Destroyed by the beat of the next,
Crying *My name was writ in water.*
We know too the myth of our self-destructiveness
The slide into a needle, the cave of fur,
The singer shattered like his smashed guitar.
We were raised on it.
These stories must comfort someone.
Yet other artists continue lives of disciplined labor
Invent strategies to defy the failing eyes,
The weakening arm,
Work larger, simpler, more enraged, or more serene.
Writers sometimes grunt into their eighties
Not necessarily growing witless.
Certain women survive
Their erotic petals and pollen, grasp dirt, bite stone
Muttering *I can't go on, I'll go on*
—No knowing which script applies to us.

That it was we who fed the children language,
That the juice and joy of their growth was ours,
That when they suffered it was we who staggered
Defeated by useless unglamorous grief,
We whom responsibility drove mad, years at a shot
Unable to create, taking to our beds,
To our exhausted pills,
That our yearning for them would be ineradicable,
That we would drone about their whiffs of nectar,
Even when they scorned us—Jewish mothers—
Everyone knows this familiar plot, but not
The secret premise. Not how it comes out.

iii

To whom shall we pray
O God of life
Inscribe us in the book of life.
The leaves grow amber, golden, brass,
We walk along the bay, sit on the dock,
Watch ripples spread where a mallard lifts,
My pockets heavy as always
With clicking beach stones.

To be a Jew meant food,
A style of irony, a taste for kindness.
Violin tremolos. We used to think so.
We, the never-included, who believed
God meant the promise, *They shall not hurt nor destroy*
In all my holy mountain.
Today women who gather to pray aloud
By the warm stones of the Western Wall
In the holy city of Jerusalem
Have chairs flung at them, curses spit.
They are called whores
By some who call themselves people of God,
People of the book. A prime
Minister ascends to microphones

Through the sharp wailing of the Intifada
To declaim of those whose lives are in his power
They are as grasshoppers to us
If they dare defy us,
Their children's heads dashed against stones.

In Prague when you asked the doorkeeper
At the Old Synagogue for admission
He said, "Ask in Hebrew," and you could not.
He said, "Ask in Yiddish," and you still could not,
And he refused you.
Who is this God who refuses,
What does the book of life want to tell us.

Uphill your house holds sculpture in every room,
Bronze, silver, gifts to the future, a register
Of pain and anger poured into ugly beauty.
The body's loop from clay to clay.
Even as a student, when they said, *Sweetheart,*
Figurative sculpture is dead, you set your jaw
To the perfect formal value of stubbornness,
Another tribal urge, like problem solving—
When the problem is too difficult—
Il faut toujours travailler, said Rodin.
A young woman, a dancer, in leotards
Buttocks of bronze solidly planted
On a high stool, gaze bold and fearful.
Your elderly aunt, palms on trousered knees,
Bronze breasts drooping in T-shirt,
Practical, frank, undeluded.
Youth, knees wide open, testicles
A temptation to a woman's palm,
Patina gunmetal gray as we enter the kitchen.
Archaic figured mirrors, moon-women,
Bound women, women in tears, bulblike
Until one climbs as from imprisonment
Or from a pod, her silvered clitoris

A signal of freedom.
Plaques of a face, your own, much magnified,
Whose fist shadows a stare of brutal rudeness.
The daughter and her girlfriend, caught
Forever in their insolent teens
Are like opened irises.
Hammered metal hair streams down their backs.
The scientist, your husband's colleague
Whom you admire, shambling hands in pockets,
Face blent intelligence and mischief,
Figure an equivalent of his Yorkshire burr.
A bust of our dead friend, bald as she became,
Which it hurt you so much to complete.

In the studio eight feet tall
A goddess still in plaster
Begins at the cleft, ascends through belly, breasts,
To a face again your own, yet strangely calm.
There will be three of this one,
Each a pillar. *Doth not wisdom cry? and understanding
Put forth her voice?* After that, three flying women
Like branches of one tree
Gathered by wind,
Sketched already on the armature.
Can't work? Too afraid,
Tired, guilty?
*She is a tree of life to them that lay hold of her
For wisdom is better than rubies.*
                                        If the task
As time flies is to press the spirit forth
Unrepentant, struggling to praise
Our hopeless bodies, our hopeless world,
What is required? What pools of luck?
Inscribe us in the book of life.
Perhaps we already know
Where to direct such a prayer.

iv

You started the eight-foot goddess
The year Cynthia spent dying,
The same year you were sculpting
Her small bald head
Fretting you couldn't get
The form. Like all your portraits
It was a compound of yourself and her.
Your zinnias hold out longer than anyone's.
You've planted them where
Extra sun seems to collect
A golden pool near your back kitchen stair.

v

When we think, not of death
But of the decay before it—before us—
I ask you at high noon, who doesn't flinch?
What if there is a season for everything?
Autumn mornings I hear my brain cells pop
One by one, emitting gentle sighs
Like the bubbles in plastic wrapping.
I conjure the stroke, the aphasia,
The nursing home wheelchairs they'll strap me to,
All of me smooth and numb as scar tissue,
The tubes invading my essential holes.
They call me sweet buttercup, dear little buttercup,
I sang that once in *Pinafore*. But a vegetable?
A wilted lettuce?
Or even some crooked wisp
Taken for her daily walk
By a strong brown woman on eraser shoes
—And suddenly you turn and say to me
Whoever we are, we'll be to the end.

Like our friend who died, having decided
No more chemo, no heroic measures.
Lingering? Fuck that, she said.

Morphine for the pain, against the pain.
That final day, her daughters assembled
As she slept and woke, slept and moaned.
They made the decision to switch
To the intravenous. It was morphine all the way then.
All night they waked and watched her sleep
And said from time to time, as she almost surfaced,
She'd sing a line from one of the folk songs
On her Elektra records, that she recorded
When they were kids
And she was almost famous,
As if to sing herself back to sleep,
Then sank again, rose and sank.

Both of us can still reproduce
The downward inflection with which Cynthia would say
In her vibrant near-baritone voice
Sheeeeit, or Fuuuuck.
We remember her tallness of stature,
Elegant costumes—I coveted in particular
A pair of butter-soft, cherry red
Italian gloves.
We recall her tragicomic love affairs,
Her taste in flowers, Catalan cooking,
Shelves of tattered blues and flamenco records.
She used to describe the folk music scene in America
—*Before money made a hole in it*
And the joy spilled out.
Integrity unobscured by death

Is what we hope for, then.
But to whom should we say
Inscribe me in the book of life.

To whom if not each other
To whom if not our damaged children
To whom if not our piteous ancestors

To whom if not the lovely ugly forms
We have created,
The forms we wish to coax
From the clay of nonexistence—
However persistent the voice
That rasps *hopeless,* that claims
Your fault, your fault—
As if outside the synagogue we stood
On holier ground in a perennial garden
Jews like ourselves have just begun to plant.

✌ Middle-Aged Woman at a Pond

The first of June, grasses already tall
In which I lie with a book. All afternoon a cardinal
Has thrown the darts of his song.

One lozenge of sun remains on the pond,
The high crowns of the beeches have been transformed
By a stinging honey. *Tell me,* I think.

Frogspawn floats in its translucent sacs.
Tadpoles rehearse their crawls.
Here come the blackflies now,

And now the peepers. This is the nectar
In the bottom of the cup,
This blissfulness in which I strip and dive.

Let my questions stand unsolved
Like trees around a pond. Water's cold lick
Is a response. I swim across the ring of it.

✌ The Nature of Beauty

> I can only say, there we have been; but I cannot say *where.*
> —*T. S. Eliot*

As sometimes whiteness forms in a clear sky
To represent the breezy, temporary
Nature of beauty,
Early in semester they started it.
Lisa read in her rich New Jersey accent,
Which mixes turnpike asphalt with fast food,
A sexy poem that mentioned "the place
Where lovers go to when their eyes are closed
And their lips smiling." Other students grinned,
Thinking perhaps of the backseats of Hondas.
Instead of explaining "place" as a figure of speech,
The teacher wanted them to crystallize
Around it as around the seed of a cloud.
You all understand that? You understand?
The place we go to? Where we've been? They got it.

All semester they brought it back
A piece at a time, like the limbs of Osiris.
Mostly from sex, for they were all American
Nineteen to twenty-one year olds
Without a lot of complicated notions.
But Doug got it from the Jersey shore,
Foam stroking his shins, his need
Leaping in fish form. Robin
One time from dancing
With a woman she didn't
Have sex with, once from her grandmother
Doing the crossword puzzle in pen.
Kindly David from a monstrous orange bus
Whose driver amazed him by kindliness
To passengers who were poor and demented.
Dylan from a Baptist church when song
Blent him into its congregation, sucked him

Into God, for a sanctified quarter hour,
"There's no separation at that height,"
Before it dropped him like Leda back to earth
And the perplexity of being white.

The vapor of the word collects,
Becomes cloud, pours itself out,
Almost before you think: the small
Rain down can rain.
A brief raid on the inarticulate
Is what we get, and in retreat we cannot
Tell where we've really been, much less remain.

The Class

We say things in this class. Like why it hurts.
But what they say outside of class is different; worse.
The teacher hears tales from the combat zone
Where the children live, conscripted at birth,
In dynamited houses. Like all draftees,
They have one job, survival,
And permit themselves some jokes.
Like my father hits the bottle . . .
And my mother. In my office a sofa,
Books, prints, disorder on the desk.
Everything paid for, chosen, they know that.
I've put myself in a drug rehab program
Or *I know I'm anorexic* or *The sonofabitch*
Was raping me for years and now
I'm so frightened for my little sister
But she refuses to talk to me.
Their nervous eyes glide over printed poems
I hand them, but nothing exactly sticks—
The black student pulled apart by his loyalties
Whose bravado breaks like a shoelace
At a cleaning man's curse, *you fuckin' Oreo.*
The homosexual drummer tapping out
A knee tune, wagging his Groucho brows.
Hey, you ought to meet my mom real soon.
'Cause when I tell her, she's gonna die.
Abuse, attempted suicide, incest,
Craziness, these are common stories,
This is street-to-street fighting
Yet these children are privileged.
They're eating.
They have their own beds, and they go to college.

The teacher's job is to give them permission
To gather pain into language, to insist
The critics are wrong, the other professors are wrong
Who describe an art divisible from dirt,
From rotten life. *You have to,*
Of course, you have to write it. What the hell
Do you think Emily did, Walt did, Hart did,
Bill did, Sylvia did. Write for your own sake,
Write for the sake of the silenced,
Write what makes you afraid to write.
The teacher hates the job. She'd like to make
The classroom a stopping-place in a pilgrimage,
Poetry itself a safe-house
Between slavery and freedom.
Since that is impossible,
Since "freedom" is another word
Like "foot" and "ankle" to the amputee,
The teacher helps them descend to hell,
Where she cannot reach them, where books are ashes,
Where language is hieroglyphs carved in walls
Running with slime, which they'll have to feel for
In the steamy mist, while the whip opens their backs.
They'll write about that, or nothing.
Against evidence, the teacher believes
Poetry heals, or redeems suffering,
If we can enter its house of judgment.
Perhaps it is not the poet who is healed,
But someone else, years later.
The teacher tells herself that truth is powerful.
Great is truth, and mighty above all things,
Though she would never say so in a class.

✒ Locker Room Conversation

There are some men my husband never sees
With their pants on, though they work at the same
University, guys from other departments.
Men, it seems, don't bother wearing towels
In the locker room; though at his age there's often
Plenty to hide, he and his buddies have eyed each other
For so many years, on and off the squash court,
What would be the point? In the shower they chat
About their games, about the last op-ed,
Or they gossip and tell jokes and do business.
He likes to describe this camaraderie
And I like to imagine the naked men
In their various stages of beauty and decay
Splashing, surrounded by brightly falling water—
The muscular definition of smooth youth,
The humorous pouchiness of the middle aged,
The crisp ligaments of the old, that squashy layer
Of boy-fat under the skin at last consumed,
Their bodies like engravings you could title
"Persistence" or "Integrity,"
And sometimes even the very old,
Softened again like very old wool,
All showering in a hum of conversation.

He likes to mention some of the specimens
I would enjoy—The big-necked boy athletes,
The Indian M.D. in his fifties, graceful as Shiva.
Today he tells me someone he's never seen
Walked into the shower, a kid, near seven feet,
Black curly hair, bronze, except for a bikini mark,
Blue eyes, face of an angel, body of a Greek hero,
Thighs the circumference of my husband's waist,

Dong of a god; and conversation stopped.
Every man just soaped and rinsed himself.
Afterward, as they dressed, my husband asked
A couple of friends.—What did you think of that guy?
—What guy, they said.

Jonah's Gourd Vine

Outside Papyrus Books, Upper Broadway,
The street person in faded sweatpants,
A crackled bomber jacket and missing teeth,
Big handsome man the color of ripe
Aubergines, having laid down a khaki
Parka at the angle of the building,
Admonishes his dog. Sit! Don't sit on the sidewalk!
You'll catch cold! Sit! Sit on the raincoat.
Passersby notice how he's dressed the dog
In a frayed sweater, everyone thinks it's
Heartwarming. Minutes later, though,
I'm inside the bookstore, and he's staggering,
Roaring something quite other, angrily
Over and over up and down the street,
Threats, imprecations, curses it sounds like,
As if the world were coming to an end
And he wanted his voice to bring it down,
So that the girl at the cash register
Murmurs to the assistant in the shop
—That one, I mean it, he's really obnoxious.
Jangles her bracelets and rolls her eyes.
—*Es muy loco,* agrees the other. They make
Red Puerto Rican downturned mouths, while I
Pay for my copy of Zora Neale Hurston's
Jonah novel, thinking how we're all
Here in Nineveh, that great wicked town,
But no sign yet we're ready to repent.

Still Life: A Glassful of Zinnias on My Daughter's Kitchen Table

i

In the interminable quest for truth
For the facts as perceived
What has to be included—

The zinnias, in the act—I need
To pay attention—tusking rich golden
Petals in layers, rings, the central rows tipped auburn,
Built blossoms whose spiky digits were still at that moment releasing
Their clasp of a polleny core which others still clung to,
Ravishing unconscious golden petals,
But what I also saw
Immediately was
The tangle of flabby leaves, that seemed
The green of old and sagging uniforms
Like cloth laundered to a shabby softness
Sorrowful as the inside of my arm
Crowded and in the process
Of dying, perhaps conscious of it too,
But only later, while drawing the whole mass
In pencil in my sketchbook
And so truly paying attention
Did I notice the buds
Their wrapped repeating patterns
Their sullen spheres like fists
With darkened auburn tips
Surrounded, as they opened or were soon to open,
By thin rigorous leaves, sentinels
Guarding a family of royal youngsters,
Only then exactly to understand
What I see in this tangle is all process
All fierce birth maturity decline
Of some zinnias ripped
From a bush

And this is only one
Glassful of zinnias
And this is only one
Soliloquy

So shall I mention my daughter only married
One month ago
Mention flowering up and down the street
In Berkeley January
Mention a gray green-eyed cat
A lemon tree on the corner
Eucalyptus in the hills
Raining their scent

And this is only one soliloquy

ii

What the eye instantly consents to
Language stumbles after
Like some rejected
Clumsy perpetual lover, language
Encouraging himself: maybe this time
She'll go with me, she'll be nice
And sometimes she does and is, she swivels
Like a powdered blonde on the next bar stool
And turns around upon her glorious flanks,
She is kind to him
And he explodes, he's out of his skin
With foolish pleasure—

It never lasts, however!

So in contrast with the intensity of the hard
Buds, pulling themselves open,
And on the other hand the grief
Of the flabby dying leaves, comes the unconscious
Soaring blossoms' thickened glory

—Consciousness driving itself until it yields
Narcosis of full being, the golden blossoms
The petals of unconsciousness, which in turn break down
At the advent of decay
The very cells break down
Into thought, curling,
Gloomily ironic—
The very cells break down, their membranes crushed
And are dragged, as to a prison

Where the condemned
Beg for forgetfulness
Where the guards
Revel in brutality

iii

Table in the middle of the dining room
Clear grain, a stack of magazines, chipped dishes,
The band of sunlight diagonal on the dusty floor,
The thick telephone book, the daughter at school
Having plunged into it, her existence, having begun to swim hard,
The daughter's husband dreamily at work across the bay,
The mother dreaming also, pencil in hand.

A glassful of zinnias on the table.

Berkeley, January 18, 1990

Excerpts from "The Mastectomy Poems"

The Bridge

You never think it will happen to you,
What happens every day to other women.
Then as you sit paging a magazine,
Its beauties lying idly in your lap,
Waiting to be routinely waved good-bye
Until next year, the mammogram technician
Says *Sorry, we need to do this again,*

And you have already become a statistic,
Citizen of a country where the air,
Water, your estrogen, have just saluted
Their target cells, planted their Judas kiss
Inside the Jerusalem of the breast.
Here on the film what looks like specks of dust
Is calcium deposits.
Go put your clothes on in a shabby booth
Whose curtain reaches halfway to the floor.
Try saying *fear*. Now feel
Your tongue as it cleaves to the roof of your mouth.

Technicalities over, medical articles read,
Decisions made, the Buick's wheels
Nose across Jersey toward the hospital
As if on monorail. Elizabeth
Exhales her poisons, Newark Airport spreads
Her wings—the planes take off over the marsh—
A husband's hand plays with a ring.

Some snowflakes whip across the lanes of cars
Slowed for the tollbooth, and two smoky gulls
Veer by the steel parabolas.
Given a choice of tunnel or bridge
Into Manhattan, the granite crust
On its black patter of rivers, we prefer
Elevation to depth, vista to crawling.

Riddle: Post-Op

A-tisket a-tasket
I'm out of my casket
Into my hospital room
With a view of Riverside Drive
Where the snow is a feathery shawl
My children plump as chestnuts by the fire
My son-in-law so humorous and tall
My mate grandly solicitous, a broker
With a millionaire's account.
My friends bob in
And out like apples
Crying and crying *You look wonderful*
While underneath this posh new paisley
Bathrobe that laps me in luxury
Underneath my squares of gauze
I've a secret, I've a riddle
That's not a chestful of medals
Or a jeweled lapel pin
And not the trimly sewn
Breast pocket of a tailored business suit
It doesn't need a hanky
It's not the friendly slit of a zipper
Or a dolphin grin
Or a kind word from the heart
Not a twig from a dogwood tree
Not really a worm
Though you could have fooled me
It was not drawn with crayon
Brushed on with watercolor
Or red ink,
It makes a skinny stripe
That won't come off with soap
A scarlet letter lacking a meaning
Guess what it is
It's nothing

Mastectomy

—for Allison Estabrook

I shook your hand before I went.
Your nod was brief, your manner confident,
A ship's captain, and there I lay, a chart
Of the bay, no reefs, no shoals.
While I admired your boyish freckles,
Your soft green cotton gown with the oval neck,
The drug sent me away, like the unemployed.
I swam and supped with the fish, while you
Cut carefully in, I mean
I assume you were careful.
They say it took an hour or so.

I liked your freckled face, your honesty
That first visit, when I said
What's my odds on this biopsy
And you didn't mince words,
One out of four it's cancer.
The degree on your wall shrugged slightly.
Your cold window onto Amsterdam
Had seen everything, bums and operas.
A breast surgeon minces something other
Than language.
That's why I picked you to cut me.

Was I succulent? Was I juicy?
Flesh is grass, yet I dreamed you displayed me
In pleated paper like a candied fruit,
I thought you sliced me like green honeydew
Or like a pomegranate full of seeds
Tart as Persephone's, those electric dots
That kept that girl in hell,
Those jelly pips that made her queen of death.
Doctor, you knifed, chopped, and divided it
Like a watermelon's ruby flesh

Flushed a little, serious
About your line of work
Scooped up the risk in the ducts
Scooped up the ducts
Dug out the blubber,
Spooned it off and away, nipple and all.
Eliminated the odds, nipped out
Those almost insignificant cells that might
Or might not have lain dormant forever.

What fed my daughters, my son
Trickles of bliss,
My right guess, my true information,
What my husband sucked on
For decades, so that I thought
Myself safe, I thought love
Protected the breast.
What I admired myself, liking
To leave it naked, what I could
Soap and fondle in its bath, what tasted
The drunken airs of summer like a bear
Pawing a hive, half up a sycamore.
I'd let sun eyeball it, surf and lake water
Reel wildly around it, the perfect fit,
The burst of praise. Lifting my chin
I'd stretch my arms to point it at people,
Show it off when I danced. I believed this pride
Would protect it, it was a kind of joke
Between me and my husband
When he licked off some colostrum
Even a drop or two of bitter milk
He'd say *You're saving for your grandchildren.*

I was doing that, and I was saving
The goodness of it for some crucial need,
The way a woman
Undoes her dress to feed
A stranger, at the end of *The Grapes of Wrath,*
A book my mother read me when I was
Spotty with measles, years before
The breast was born, but I remembered it.
How funny I thought goodness would protect it.
Jug of star fluid, breakable cup—

Someone shoveled your good and bad crumbs
Together into a plastic container
Like wet sand at the beach,
For breast tissue is like silicon.
And I imagined inland orange groves,
Each tree standing afire with solid citrus
Lanterns against the gleaming green,
Ready to be harvested and eaten.

December 31

I say this year no different
From any other, so we party, the poets
And physicists arrive bearing
Cheeses, chile, sesame noodles,
Meats, mints, whatever—
Champagne—
Filling up the sideboard,
Filling the house up, filling it.
At midnight everyone kisses,
My man replenishes
His wicked punch,
My mother folk dances,
In the kitchen they pass a joint,
Then after that they put
The hard rock on,
And I, dressed
In black tights and a borrowed
Black and red China silk jacket,
Am that rolling stone, that
Natural woman

No different, no
Different, and by 3 A.M. if
The son of my blood
And the wild student of my affection
Should choose to carry on, if
My goddess daughter with her satiric
Stringbean boyfriend
Tuck themselves into the bunk
Bed of her girlhood, may they hear me
Mutter in sleep, sleep
Well and happy
New year.

Wintering

> i had expected more than this.
> i had not expected to be
> an ordinary woman.
> —*Lucille Clifton*

It snows and stops, now it is January,
The houseplants need feeding,
The guests have gone. Today I'm half a boy,
Flat as something innocent, a clean
Plate, just needing a story.
A woman should be able to say
I've become an Amazon,
Warrior woman minus a breast,
The better to shoot arrow
after fierce arrow,
Or else *I am that dancing Shiva*
Carved in the living rock at Elephanta,
One-breasted male deity, but I don't feel
Holy enough or mythic enough.
Taking courage, I told a man *I've resolved*
To be as sexy with one breast
As other people are with two
And he looked away.

Spare me your pity,
Your terror, your condolence.
I'm not your wasting heroine,
Your dying swan. Friend, tragedy
Is a sort of surrender.
Tell me again I'm a model
Of toughness. I eat that up.
I grade papers, I listen to wind,
My husband helps me come, it thaws
A week before semester starts.

Now Schubert plays, and the tenor wheels
Through Heine's lieder. A fifteen-year survivor
Phones: *You know what? You're the same person
After a mastectomy as before.* An idea
That had never occurred to me.
*You have a job you like? You have poems to write?
Your marriage is okay? It will stay that way.
The wrinkles are worse. I hate looking in the mirror.
But a missing breast, well, you get used to it.*

Normal

First classes, the sun is out, the darlings
Troop in, my colleagues
Tell me I look normal. I am normal.
The falsie on my left makes me
In a certain sense more perfectly normal.
An American who lives beyond my means,
A snake-oil foot in the door,
A politician with a strong
Handshake in an election year.
Crafted of latex, it repairs the real.
Like one of those trees with a major limb lopped,
I'm a shade more sublime today than yesterday.
Stormed at with shot and shell,
A symbol of rich experience,
A scheme to outlive you all.

Meanwhile a short piece of cosmic string
Uncoiled from the tenth dimension
Has fastened itself to my chest.
Ominous asp, it burns and stings,
Grimaces to show it has no idea
How it arrived here.
Would prefer to creep off.
Yet it is pink and smooth as gelatin.
It will not bite, and can perhaps be tamed.
Want to pet it? It cannot hurt you.
Care to fingertip my silky scar?

Now I am better, charming. I am well.
Yes, I am quite all right. I never say
The thing that is forbidden to say,
Piece of meat, piece of shit.
Cooled, cropped, I'm simple and pure.
Never invite my colleagues
To view it pickled in a Mason jar.

Healing

Brilliant—
A day that is less than zero
Icicles fat as legs of deer
Hang in a row from the porch roof
A hand without a mitten
Grabs and breaks one off—
A brandished javelin
Made of sheer
Stolen light
To which the palm sticks
As the shock of cold
Instantly shoots through the arm
To the heart—
I need a language like that,
A recognizable enemy, a clarity—
I do my exercises faithfully,
My other arm lifts,
I apply vitamin E,
White udder cream
To the howl
I make vow after vow.

Epilogue: Nevertheless

The bookbag on my back, I'm out the door.
Winter turns to spring
The way it does, and I buy dresses.
A year later, it gets to where
When they say *How are you feeling,*
With that anxious look on their faces,
And I start to tell them the latest
About my love life or my kids' love lives,
Or my vacation, or my writer's block—
It actually takes me a while
To realize what they have in mind—
I'm fine, I say, *I'm great, I'm clean.*
The bookbag on my back, I have to run.

Uncollected and New Poems
(1980–1998)

✒ April One

Who would have thought this shrivell'd heart
Would have recover'd greenness?
—*George Herbert*

Can't believe it
A million New Jersey hearts whispering rain rain go away
For four days straight
So then it snowed
That was bizarre but that was yesterday
Today the divine old man and the divine old woman
Are holding up the tent of the sky
To let sunlight in and fresh fresh air
Can't believe it, it makes me even love Princeton,
Even me love Princeton,
Where of course there are no crocuses in *my* yard yet today
But all up Prospect where I bike to the library
In other people's yards there are excellent crocuses
In clumps and clusters like schoolgirls
Giggling and straightening their spines
When somebody passes so their pointy breasts will show
And isn't that good enough
Isn't it good the wetness is drying so fast today it's
As if robbers took it under their armpits and ran
Plus absolutely redbuds
Abruptly born and where the library doesn't say
Welcome, oho, welcome
Alicia, my pigeon, I am your tidy sanctuary, your familiar
Teacherly cocoon, your protection—no, it's horrible, it smells
Like corpses, it smells like mildew
Bless it, it shoves me out
Into the plentiful breeze
So I can look some more, not at the George Segal
Abraham about to slay Isaac in poignant life-size bronze
Commemorating the holy slaughter
Of the young by the withered fanatic old
But instead where youthful people have popped out
In bunches and throw loops of invigorating glances

In all directions at each other, weaving
The intangible web of sex until
I feel capacious and insatiable as the sea
Seeking blue eyes like Paul Newman's
Brown beards to drown in me. I am a cup
That runneth over full of empty happiness
Ready to be grateful
To all the men who ever made me happy
I hope I did them some permanent good
The women and children too

And my other children, my students,
The ones who are not idiotic, who write poetry like whipped cream
Like clouds when you look at clouds from an airplane window
After a gin and tonic and a half
The ones who understand Conrad and Margaret Atwood
Keats and Emily Dickinson, after great pain
A formal feeling comes, so when you are happy
You want to take your clothes off
And defy grammar and punctuation, I can't
Believe it today I am not flipping through
My grievance cards, no poverty,
No torture, no arms buildup, no corporate executive bathrooms,
No bone to pick with my husband that might choke me in future,
No foolish President, I am feeding
Nobody my anger dog food
I am in my middle
Forties, this is the middle of my poem
And I am remembering my nation is not at war
And I have to bicycle some more. I bicycle down
Witherspoon Street to my mother's house
To return her poems
And tell her I loved them
Sincerely, can't believe it
Chit chat, chit chat about her flowers
Her immortal future kohlrabi.
Then I have to go home and I haven't stopped

Smiling and on Leigh Street two young black men are under
A jacked-up Pontiac
My favorite springtime image, human and metal, since brass
Nor stone like the library nor something nor boundless sea
But sad mortality o'ersways its power, oh yeah
How with this rage shall beauty hold a plea (cop a plea?
Must be a legal metaphor in here)
How with this rage shall beauty hold a plea
Whose action is no stronger than a flower
Oh, Willie, baby, I'd like to tell you how
Today without effort
I am this blue-veined crocus
Straightening up on her spine
Today without effort I uphold my half of the sky
Because here is the way it is all over New Jersey:
In the tops of the redbud trees
Small boys are playing ball
In the pink light
And under the ground
Even the lost people are combing their hair.

      April 1, 1980

From the Prado Rotunda: The Family of Charles IV, and Others

Francisco José de Goya y Lucientes
Wishes to inform the universe that it can eat his name.
That it can kiss his finger. He stuffs
The Spanish arrogance of his name
Between your teeth.
Like the ugly royal bodies, it is a stiff sponge of blood,
Gold-beaded. Immobilized by garments. Streaks of stupidity
And pride marble it like meat. You chew and grimace.

He desires the form of this painting to be that of a boa constrictor
Swallowing a Pekingese. He desires the lumps to be visible
And the digestion difficult.

Is it not, remarked Hemingway, *a masterpiece of loathing?*
Look how he painted his spittle into every face.
Wan courtiers attend these monarchs, a king
Corpulent and hesitant, a queen whose large arms
Stand akimbo, poodle teeth grinning, called by Gautier
The corner baker and his wife after they have won the lottery,
Whose fatuousness blinds them from seeing flesh, face, form
As very signifiers of the painter's disgust

—with his own ambition?
Himself at work in corners of society portraits
Painting like a courteous animal, despising retouching, forcing
Their homage. What a man will do to possess the respect
Of the gilded worm. Do their commissions choke him?
Is it that hope itself wishes to melt? Whose flesh? What ceremony?
Viscera, witchery, whippings.
The silent shriek of a man in *The Madhouse*
Flees from an oval aperture black as doubt
To re-embody itself a century later
In bourgeois Norway.

Inaudible owls crowd the sleep of Reason,
Saturn devours children
In fact. Fact.

The densest element in the periodic table is lead.
Attempting to lift a box you might hemorrhage.
The painting of Goya is denser than lead,
The painting is insupportable.
If he is leading us by the hand like babes
To worship the abject monstrous because it exists, to sniff
Hysteria from within like an infection
Among the tambourines and the fans and the mantillas,
If Goya's lascivious Maja
Nude and clothed in the duplicity
Native to women
Makes your mouth water—
If her pale legs flow strangely together
As if glued to a board they cannot bend at the knee,
As if returning to fishtails—

The painting is never what is *there,*
It throbs with the mystery
Of your own sick-to-death soul
Which demands, like everything alive,
Love.

A Chinese Fan Painting

It is late afternoon, the cherries bloom.
The master returns to his mountain pavilion
After a great absence.
Donkey trots him over bridge,
Burdened servant follows with lantern,
A child runs up stone steps from the river
Carrying two jars,
A dog comes forth to meet the master.

A little banner on a pole
Shows how the wind blows.
And this is all on silk.

The foreground cliffs with bristling pines
Argue for nature's solidity, the background
Mountains half in mist argue against
This and many other illusions.
Tree limbs, rocks, river, bridge, pavilion.
Browns, greens, washes and accents.
Tiny pink dots—
Cherry trees blooming in both the worlds.

🦢 O'Keeffe

New York: you are staring safely down from Steiglitz's apartment
At a tub and three trees in someone's garden.
In a single warm, dusty afternoon
Under your eyes the magnolia buds
Have swollen up like fetuses.

You watch them prepare their scent.

They are like generals in a windowless map room
Who summarize plans an hour before a battle
And you also are not yet unspooled,
Girl, and the century is
New enough—America has not yet shown her fist,
It is only 1916—her midwestern vibrant fist.

A square format like a boxing ring.
A cat asleep among hollyhocks.
There is tension and excitement, a horse clip-clops
Somewhere out on the street in its timeless way
And an aide nods and salutes and the men shake hands.

You have not yet said *There is nothing less real than realism.*
The air grows hotter and more still.
One magnolia opens her taffeta skirt.

❧ Anselm Kiefer

At the border between reality and the imagination

No soldiers, no machine guns

Only rutted mud stubbled as after harvest
And from chimneys over the horizon the pale sky
Receives a faint, almost imperceptible stain

But you and your companions are in no danger
Although if you were here by moonlight you might be frightened
By the sheets of unstoppable brightness

The combination of metal and earth
The convergence toward a vanishing point
The absence of nocturnal birds

Not here but eastward the border goes through a forest
You would be more frightened there, out of the open
Where it is truly opaque and entangling, many become lost

As if swept away by history

The border lies a kilometer ahead
The gilded engine that delivered you returns
Murmuring to its anarchic city

The rails battered to silence behind your back—

❧ Holocaust

—*From* holokaustos, *burnt offering*

Fire: a rapid, persistent chemical reaction that releases heat and light, esp. the exothermic combination of a combustible substance with oxygen. Intensity, as of feeling. Ardor. Enthusiasm. Luminosity or brilliance, as of a cut and polished gemstone. Liveliness and vivacity of imagination, inspiration. A torment, trial, or tribulation. The discharge of firearms.

And about burning people—
They were never wrong, the old
Old masters,

How it never stopped, it is done all the time,
How you must admit there is an absolute
Seductiveness, a classic primal urge—

Is not my word like as a fire?

Oh Jephthah's daughter, ah Joan,
Oh Jews and Protestants, ah Sir Thomas More,
Oh Giordano Bruno, ah heretics, witches, fanatics—

Scent of magnolia sweet and fresh
In the Carolina woods, a splash of gasoline
And the sudden smell of burning flesh

Oh Jericho, ah Carthage,
Oh Hiroshima,
Masses at once, masses

In the fiery patriotic mind,
Men stroking themselves
Eyes half shut, women aroused,

You as a child first feeling that excitement
At the cave mouth—
Sparks flying upward to emulate stars

You dancing to emulate the fierce commotion
Your mouth greasy after eating
Running with the dogs round the circle

The hiss, the crackle, the boom, the fragrance—
The sweet savor—

You draw close enough to set
Two hard fires ablaze in your two eyes
And they never go out—

Mean little fires,
Satan's toys,
God's flames.

A rapid, persistent
Chemical
Reaction.

✌ Diaspora

i

The forsythia bush is made of yellow fire,
The daffodils are made of yellow fire,
It is why they are so difficult to look at.

To obtain your attention
They cry shrilly just beyond the capacity of your ears.
Perhaps you feel the discomfort in your sinuses
And guess that if you permitted yourself one glance

They would grip you with the tenacity
Of the wheelchair-bound elderly, or of the mad—

ii

Take the above as an allegory of learning:
Springtime, resurrection, your heritage, death and life,
Each dangerous truth you would almost prefer to refuse—

Neither does it stop here,
For already a bed of tulips holds flesh cups
Like the dead family around a child
Dressed stiffly for a first recital, a row of eyes

And a row of heaving breasts, until you see
You can never learn the routine of truth—
Were you ever wise?
If when you were children you knew, you knew—
More and more will be expected of you.

Millennial Polka

Using words this way,
Like chopped crockery—
What is it?

A release? An evacuation? Stop
Making sense,
The musicians say.

Express your anger like a swan.

A prayer, at this late date,
God, a little punch
Through your membrane?

We're only peasants here,
Kyrie eleison, we're jumping
About in the full barns

Among the bloody berries.

About Time

Rather they are joy, against nothingness joy.

—*Louis Zukovsky*

What we have been doing
The idea was—
The work of science. Of art.
The philosophical heart
Hardened. Timeless. If you strike it, it clangs. It
Beats time.

What you can't kill: the mud
And what is inside the mud
A spirit panting
Ma non troppo

The body's loop from clay to clay
Interrupted. Wrestled, made to gleam.

Under the garden
The world spirit panting
Slick, sour
Along with its worms
Each an individual
Produces a tunnel
Of air and crumbs
Humbly
       O artist
Humbly! awaiting their hour.

Until then
Already
Not yet
Soon.

Acknowledgments

This volume includes poems from the following books and chapbooks: *Songs* (Holt Rinehart and Winston, 1969); *Once More Out of Darkness, and Other Poems* (Berkeley Poets Co-op, 1974); *A Dream of Springtime: Poems 1970–77* (The Smith/Horizon Press, 1978); *The Mother-Child Papers* (Momentum Press, 1980; rpt. Beacon Press, 1986); *A Woman Under the Surface* (Princeton University Press, 1982); *The Imaginary Lover* (University of Pittsburgh Press, 1986); *Green Age* (University of Pittsburgh Press, 1989); *The Crack in Everything* (University of Pittsburgh Press, 1996).

Some of the poems not previously in these books have appeared in the following publications; *American Poetry Review; Ontario Review; Prairie Schooner; Green Mountains Review; The American Voice.* Reprinted by permission of the publishers.

I am grateful to the MacDowell Foundation for the opportunity to work on this volume. Thanks also to Maxine Kumin, Toi Derricotte, David Keller, Fredrick Tibbetts, Sheila Solomon, J. P. Ostriker, and Peter Pitzele, for helping me select and arrange the poems. Heartfelt thanks above all to my editor, Ed Ochester, for his scrupulous and generous reading and advice.

A number of these poems have been slightly revised since their first printing; some have been excerpted from longer sequences.

Alicia Suskin Ostriker is one of America's premier poets and critics. She is the author of eight previous volumes of poetry, including *The Imaginary Lover* (1986), which received the William Carlos Williams Award of the Poetry Society of America, and *The Crack in Everything* (1996), which was a National Book Award finalist and won both the Paterson Poetry Award and the San Francisco State Poetry Center Award. Ostriker's most recent critical works include *Feminist Revision and the Bible* and *The Nakedness of the Fathers: Biblical Visions and Revisions.*